LILLIAN

TOO's

irresistible

book of feng shui magic

LILLIAN TOO's

irresistible
book of feng shui magic

*48 sure ways to create magic
in your living space*

ELEMENT

A graduate of the Harvard Business School in Boston, Lillian Too put her MBA to excellent use as managing director of banking and retail giants in Hong Kong during a highly successful business career in the 1980s. Upon leaving the big business forum, she returned to Malaysia to spend more time with her family and to devote her abundant energy to writing, specifically on Feng Shui, a subject she made uniquely her own in the 1990s. Her books on the subject have penetrated every corner of the globe, and she has made the bestseller lists in the USA, the UK, Germany Holland, Norway, and South Africa. Her previous books include *The Illustrated Encyclopedia of Feng Shui, The Complete Illustrated Guide to Feng Shui, The Complete Illustrated Guide to Feng Shui for Gardens,* the Feng Shui *Fundamentals* series, *Lillian Too's Little Book of Feng Shui* and *Lillian Too's Smart Feng Shui for the Home.*

Lillian lives in Kuala Lumpur, where she observes the principles of Feng Shui in her own home and immediate environment, and devotes her time to her daughter, Jennifer; to writing her own books; contributing to numerous magazines; and running her own publishing company – all of which she does with marked success.

Lillian Too's author website is: www.lillian-too.com
The World's leading Feng Shui website is: www.wofs.com
The World's largest Feng Shui E-store is: www.fsmegamall.com
Free Feng Shui E-greeting cards and screensavers: www.fsgreetings.com

This book is dedicated with love
to my darling daughter Jennifer.

Element
An Imprint of HarperCollinsPublishers
77–85 Fulham Palace Road
Hammersmith, London W6 8JB

The website address is: www.elementbooks.com

First published in Great Britain in 2001 by
Element Books Limited

10 9 8 7 6 5 4 3 2 1

Text copyright © Lillian Too, 2001
Copyright © HarperCollinsPublishers, 2001

Lillian Too asserts the moral right to
be identified as the author of this work

Illustrations by Joan Corlass
Design by Liz Brown
Project Editor: Liz Dean

A catalogue record for this book
is available from the British Library

ISBN 0 00 711701 9

Printed and bound in Great Britain by
Scotprint, Haddington, East Lothian

SAFETY NOTE

Please note that the rituals in this book are designed to be practiced by
adults and are not suitable for children. It is the responsibility of the
individual to perform rituals safely, particularly those involving mirrors.

Therefore, neither the publisher nor author can be held accountable for any
accident or injury, whether physical or mental, resulting from the practice
and interpretation of the information in this book.

contents

Introduction

We use the word magic to describe phenomena we do not understand...

To those ignorant of what has been invented in the last 100 years, commercial aircraft, lasers, digital cameras, stereo music systems, and satellite communication would appear to be powerful sorcery. The list of what is commonplace today, but would be classed as magic not so long ago, is endless. The electronic toys of the new millennium would be celestial magic in a past era but to us, now, these apparently magical phenomena can all be explained quite rationally.

But what about magic that enables people to create a better life for themselves – a lifestyle of comfort, wealth, happiness, and good fortune – by manipulating spatial and time energy patterns? Think of this "magic" as energy, life force or *chi* that mutates and transforms, creating extraordinary changes both within individuals and in the environment around them. Imagine being able to capture, store, accumulate, and manipulate this *chi* into powerful, luminous energy that illuminates and improves every aspect of life. The magic that makes this happen – Feng Shui magic – is part of a wider system of Taoist practice, which I like to call "the science of the sages." Whilst the philosophical

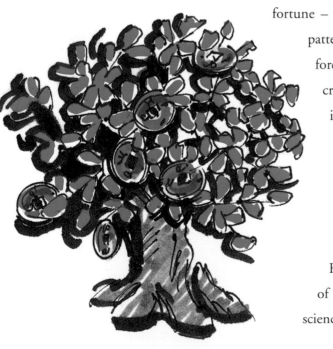

Prosperity magic can be generated with a gem tree.

Chinese wealth deities attract money luck for the household.

underpinnings of the Tao can sometimes seem lofty or profound, the techniques of Feng Shui are very specific and easier to apply.

Feng Shui magic is a prosperity-creating phenomenon that uses a number of different systems or "schools." My practice of Feng Shui combines the use of compass formulas with auspicious symbols. It is not necessarily advanced Feng Shui but it is more comprehensive, yet simpler and more exciting to practice. This is because Feng Shui magic embraces several different techniques of Feng Shui simultaneously. There is nothing sinister in Feng

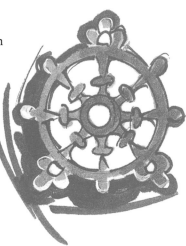

Creating a wealth vase for prosperity involves a magic ritual and secret ingredients.

The wish-balloon rituals call upon dragon magic for success.

Shui magic; it simply requires a deep understanding of the symbolism of objects, colors, seasons, foods, trigrams, elements, and so forth, along with a good working knowledge of the application of formula Feng Shui.

Included in this book are 48 techniques that will show you how to create Feng Shui magic in your life. You will learn how to increase your income by building wealth waterfalls and water flows, and applying secret water formulas. You will discover how to make, close, consecrate, and place wealth vases in your home to attract wealth luck into your living space. You will be taught the secrets of flying numbers that reveal auspicious and inauspicious corners within the home. You will learn to use healthy tree and plant energy to strengthen your body chi and recover quickly from lingering illnesses.

According to Taoist masters, the "quiet mind" – the mind that has been developed to stay calm, detached, and perfectly still – has the potential to alter the physical world exponentially if it has been used with the correct intent. I have spent several years now practicing a form of meditation that helps me to still my mind. In recent years I have focused on embracing my mind with my breath, and at the same time embracing the breath with my mind. With practice, over time, I have achieved a certain balance and focus. Anyone can do what I have done. When you are able to practice the rituals and formulas contained in this book with detached stillness you will realize a high measure of success. And

Chinese coins on an invoice bring in business, as do wealth deities.

if you can do this to the extent that even when "a mountain crumbles before your eyes you will not get startled," then you will have attained the kung fu, or expertise, required to achieve astonishing results. The secret of success lies in the genuine practice of complete detachment. It is this that imbues everything that your mind focuses on with power so that the techniques, rituals, and symbols become extensions of your mind.

The mystic knot brings never-ending love.

The pagoda brings serenity and success.

Enjoy enhancing and improving your life. Do not lose sleep over doing things correctly.

I do not promise great wealth or instant happiness. But I do promise that over time, tuning the mind to the wonders of Feng Shui magic will bring varying degrees of extra good luck. This will manifest in greater successes and less obstacles in your life that will make all the difference to your feeling of well-being.

Recall what I said about developing purity of motivation. Implement each one of the 48 techniques contained in this book one by one...and work at improving your concentration. I know that you will be surprised by the results.

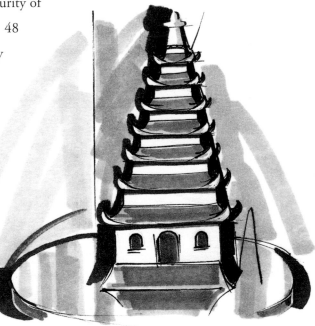

The dragon is woven into the very fabric of Chinese civilization in a shape and form that has remained remarkably unchanged over the centuries. Traditionally associated with strength and courage, the Chinese dragon has a long head with a gaping mouth, a pair of horns, and long flowing mane. His eyes are fierce and alert, his nostrils flaring, and he has a long sinewy body, covered with scales that reflect iridescent light. Sometimes the dragon is green or blue; sometimes he is red or golden. He is said to possess supernatural powers and can make himself invisible. When he flies through the skies small tongues of fire emanate from his body as he moves.

The dragon image is the most auspicious symbol in the Feng Shui gallery of propitious symbols. Activating the dragon's cosmic chi in the home can be done in many different ways depending on which Feng Shui school and which branch of Taoist teaching you wish to follow. The rituals here are based on specific tips given to me years ago while I was working in Hong Kong. At that time I was Chairman of my own chain of department stores, known as the Dragon Seed Group. I learned a great deal about the dragon then and even wrote a book about it, which I released in 1988 – the year of the dragon. The intangible power of dragon symbols has never ceased to surprise me.

one

dragon magic for success

releasing the dragon's magical
cosmic chi

For centuries the dragon has captured the imagination of humanity. In contrast to western imagery, where he is a gruesome monster to be feared and hunted, in China the dragon is a celestial creature, embodying the spirit of the earth and sky manifesting in many different forms and representing all things powerful, strong, and auspicious. Hidden among the ridges of mountains or coiled within the depths of winding waterways, his spirit bursts forth each time he is aroused. Ancient Chinese books are scattered with lyrical descriptions of his awakening. An eclipse occurs each time he decides to eat the sun or the moon, and typhoons take place when dragons battle. Dragons are believed to unfold in storm clouds, wash their scales in the waves, breathe fire as they streak through the skies like lightning, and bring the life-giving rains that mark the beginning of spring.

The dragon also plays a prominent role in Chinese history, for the Chinese dragon of antiquity descended onto earth and became the son of heaven, living as a mortal in the person of the Emperor. Whereas before he had been the ruler of the mountains and rivers, the sovereign of the seas and lord of the lakes, the dragon became a ruler of men. And so deep in the imperial halls and throne rooms of the Forbidden City in China dragons are painted, carved, engraved, and sculpted into every corner, telling eloquently of a time when dragons were revered as the highest celestial symbol of the land.

The Chinese dragon is said to possess supernatural powers. He can change color, from blue-green to golden yellow, and shape, from a mile long to a tiny earthworm, even to invisibility. He is always shown gazing

longingly or appearing to reach and touch a round elusive object, said to be the great wish-fulfilling pearl. Some view this pearl as the sun, dazzling in its brilliance, some as the moon, piercingly white in its calm and iridescent glow. Thus the dragon is said to embody cosmic chi, so that with every intangible breath of his presence he holds out the promise of a better lifestyle, the promise of unbelievable prosperity, unimaginable happiness, and the genuine awakening of the human spirit at every level – mind, body, and spirit. How much of his dragon magic materializes in your life depends as much on the quality of your practice as on your own heaven luck, or *tien chi*.

All around the world, in every country where dragons can be found, prosperity rises. Over time people living in dragon countries grow prosperous and powerful. Wealth accumulates, moving from one part of the country to another and from individual to individual. The countries that possess dragons are those with mountains. It is within the undulating ridges of a mountain range that hidden dragons build their lairs, and which, when activated, come alive bringing great prosperity and power.

Placing the dragon image inside the home represents a big part of Taoist Feng Shui magic, since it is used to activate the cosmic chi he represents. However, he has to "sit" in the correct places in the home, his eyes need to be awakened, and there are taboos associated with his size and color. He works best when placed in tandem with beautiful flowing water, and he brings great protective power to those who know how to wear his image in gold.

The American dragon spans the country with his head in California, his body writhing through Middle America, his tail in the northeastern states, and his claws spread the length of the country.

Dotting the Eyes of the Dragon

Very advanced Feng Shui adepts know how to discern the exact locations of the dragon's body across the country, and so determine the more auspicious parts that represent special spots of prosperity. They are able to tell with remarkable accuracy where to find the five claws of the dragon, where power abounds, and also the belly, where prosperity is generated. Most importantly, they can find the head and tell you where the two eyes of the dragon are situated. To date it has been a closely guarded secret, but Feng Shui experts who can locate the head and eyes of the dragon can show you how to dot the eyes of the dragon, bringing him to life. When the dragon is awakened its breath fills the surrounding environment with copious amounts of yang energy, and any home located there will enjoy tremendous good fortune.

In the past, dotting the eye of the dragon required nothing more than the strategic placement of big boulders at certain places in a village or city. This would enable the dragon to see, thereby igniting its protective powers. Today, however, many Feng Shui masters agree that boulders are insufficient. Instead, they suggest that the best method of dotting the eyes of the dragon is to build large, tall buildings at strategic points. These buildings should stay lit at all times so that they look like the eyes of the dragon when seen from the skies above. So if you believe that the American dragon has its head in California, then it is easy

Tall buildings at strategic points in cities are said to represent the eyes of the dragon.

enough to fly over the cities of Los Angeles and San Francisco to locate the buildings that symbolize the dragon's eyes. With the wealth emanating out of Silicon Valley, it seems likely that the eyes of the dragon have already been awakened.

In Hong Kong, the dragon's head is believed to be in the Tsimshatsui area, where tall, grand buildings abound. Local people maintain that there are nine dragons in this part of Hong Kong, thereby giving rise to its name Kowloon, meaning nine dragons. In Beijing, there are stunning nine-dragon walls in the Forbidden City and in the Heibei park, and in Hong Kong there is a beautiful reproduction of these walls near the waterfront in the Causeway bay area. These nine dragon walls offer celestial protection to the cities and their residents, guarding them against natural disasters.

In the Malaysian peninsula there are two dragons living along the main range of mountains. One has its head on the northeastern outskirts of Kuala Lumpur, and the other has its head on the island of Singapore, where many high-rises dotted the eyes of the peninsular dragon a couple of decades ago hence, together with other auspicious rituals and symbols, resulting in tremendous economic wealth for its people. Malaysia recently completed the Petronas twin towers, the two tallest buildings in the world, which may well represent the eyes of the Malaysian dragon.

And of course Europe is a continent that abounds with dragons. There are numerous dragons in the Alps, the most important being the five dragons emanating outward toward France, Germany, and Italy – so these and all the countries that surround the wonderful hidden abodes of fire dragons have prospered. The fortunes of European countries will surely be considerably enhanced if the major capital cities started building more skyscrapers, as this would be akin to dotting the eye of their dragons, thereby awakening them.

How to "Dot the Dragon's Eyes"

Invite the dragon into your home and dot his eyes so he comes alive. You can use porcelain, brass, or golden dragons or paintings. Do not make your dragon images too large. When the dragon overwhelms your home the chi becomes unbalanced. Also, not all homes can sustain the powerful energy of the dragon, so start modestly – dragon magic is only effective when balance is exercised. If there are people in the home born in dragon and tiger years then the dragon is more compatible with the home. But homes with people born in dog years should keep the dragon small.

Porcelain and metal dragons can have their eyes awakened with a simple but powerful ritual. Select a dragon day from the Chinese Almanac, and between 7am and 9am in the morning, the dragon hour, using a new brush and some black ink (preferably ink block) dot the eyes of your dragon. Make sure the dragon is facing east when you do this ceremony. If you have purchased a dragon painting make certain the eyes are bright and open and, when you hang it up in your home, symbolically light up the two eyes with an incense stick.

A luck-bringing dragon can be awakened by "dotting" his eyes. You can do this using a brush and black ink block.

Placement of the Dragon in the Home

Place a small dragon sculpture or painting in your living room, if possible facing east. Always use a compass to get the direction correct. A dragon can live inside or outside the home and still bring you money. A fat dragon that looks

well fed and prosperous is preferable to a thin hungry dragon, and the best image is of the dragon holding the wish-fulfilling pearl.

The dragon should always be placed facing water since the presence of yang water makes dragon symbols awaken and exude the precious breath of chi. So when you create water features in the home, like aquariums, it is a good idea to place a dragon close by. If big water – the sea, a lake, a swimming pool, or a river – is close to the home, have at least one dragon facing that body of water to bring prosperity. If you do not have any water bodies or features inside or near where you live, then place the dragon next to the kitchen sink because this water symbolizes clean water flowing in to the home.

- Never place the dragon inside the toilet or bathroom or even facing the toilet or bathroom, since this signifies that your money is being washed away. Even when the dragon is facing the sea if there is a toilet in between then symbolically the wealth has been flushed away.
- Never hang or place a dragon image in the south, the sector of Fire.
- Never position a dragon image above a fireplace since this implies that the fire energy is burning him.
- Never use a dragon carpet or rug since this is highly inauspicious. How can you succeed when you continually step on the symbol that brings success? It is for this reason that I always buy carpets with nondescript designs, or with images that mean nothing to me. Flowers and plants are good images because walking on petals and flowers denotes good fortune.
- Never have a dragon image in the bedroom, because it becomes excessively yang.

sending
wish balloons
to the sky dragons

The Chinese believe that dragons fly ever upwards and that the soaring chi of the sky dragons has the power to propel all your wishes into the cosmos. A great way to communicate your wishes to the great sky dragons is to release specially prepared wish-fulfilling balloons into the skies. Buy yourself a collection of helium-filled balloons and take them to the park or any open ground. On a slightly windy day when the sun is not too bright, look for places where beautiful clouds gather against blue skies, and let your balloons go with your wishes into the universe. This is a stunning way of attracting love into your life, improving your career prospects, and of drawing forth the great healing powers of the Universe to cure someone who is ill.

Get a black felt-tip pen and compose your message. You do not have much space on which to write, so do make certain that you construct your words carefully beforehand. If you want someone to share your life with, think through the kind of partner you want. If looks are important to you put in something that directly addresses physical appearance. If financial security is important describe that too. If you have a burning ambition, write out a description of how you see yourself. If your wish is to see someone cured, write that person's name down and describe his or her recovered state. Be as specific as you can. Remember that the goal is to send your clearly worded message into the Universe so that the winds and

Let the sky dragons make your dreams a reality. Write your wish on a yang-colored balloon, such as red or purple, and launch it into a bright blue sky.

the waters of the environment help actualize your wishes for you.

Put one wish on one balloon. This will focus the energy of the balloon on your one wish. When you have finished writing the words that best describe your heart's desire, gently release the balloon. Watch it as it flies high into the sky. When it suddenly vanishes from sight your wish has entered into the energy stream of the environment. If you have several wishes, you should send up *one* balloon at a time. If you know some mantras, chant them as you send your balloons soaring upwards; visualize them transforming into orbs of bright golden light with your message clearly emblazoned upon them.

When you have released all your balloons, forget about the wishes you have sent into the skies. Let the winds and the waters, the clouds and the sky dragons actualize your wishes for you. You will be surprised how powerful this ritual can be. It is not necessary to worry too much about your wishes once you have released your balloon. You must be careful to practice a certain detachment to the outcome of wishes, because this will enhance the strength of your messages. If you fret too much about the messages you send you will be sending out negative vibrations that could transform positive outcomes into obstacles.

dragons
as protective talismans

Belief in the spirit world and in the existence of powerful practitioners of "negative magic" is widespread in all Asian countries. This has made the use of protective talismans – often incorporating the image of the dragon and accompanied by special prayers, mantras, or magic words – an important dimension of Feng Shui practice. Different types of dragons are believed to ward off different types of negative vibration.

Wearing the Dragon Image

If you can find a gold and diamond dragon clip or a pin, wearing it correctly brings you powerful protection. Anyone can wear the dragon image and benefit from it – even those born in the year of the dog. The principal point to remember is that you should never have the dragon on your heart – so do not wear this symbol as a long pendant. However, when worn around the neck the dragon offers protection, so that a short pendant is acceptable. You can also wear the dragon as a pin or clip on your collar. For men, place the dragon on the left collar and for women, wear the dragon on the right collar. This turns the dragon into an amulet of protection, which can successfully ward off all manner of disease, illness, and accident.

Dragon rings should likewise be worn on the left hand for men and on the right hand for women. This will create powerful chi, which protects you from what are referred to as "devil men" – people who would plot against you and cause trouble behind your back. If you happen to be sleeping in a room afflicted by bad flying star numbers, wearing the dragon symbol on your body also affords you protection.

To use the dragon as an amulet or symbol of protection and good fortune, it is a good idea to differentiate between the three main types of dragons – the Tien Lung, or Sky dragon, the Shen Lung, or Sea and Rain Dragon, and the Ti Lung, or Earth dragon. Of the three, the Tien Lung dragon is acknowledged as the most powerful. He has five claws and is the imperial dragon usually drawn in gold and pictured coiling between swirls of clouds and breathing tongues of fire as he chases after the pearl. The Tien Lung brings power and nobility.

Placing an image of the Sea and Rain Dragon, Shen Lung, near water in your home brings prosperity. The Earth Dragon, Ti Lung, brings all-round good fortune. The Sky Dragon, Tien Lung, brings great power.

The Sea Dragon is the king of the four cardinal directions. He rules his domains from crystal palaces and is said to bring great wealth for those who successfully attract his presence or live near his water domains. The Shen Lung breathes foam and is often depicted blowing spouts of water. This is the dragon that brings prosperity. If you have a dragon in your home placing it near water transforms it into the Shen Lung.

The Earth dragon lives in marshland, hidden in undulating hills and mountains. It has a small neck, a hornless head, and a crimson body with a green back. Earth dragons are benevolent creatures whose powerful cosmic breath brings all-round good fortune. Having good Feng Shui automatically attracts the earth dragon's largesse. However, incurring his wrath by disturbing his veins through mindless earth digging and excavation incurs his wrath and brings grave misfortune to those who dare to do so.

Tien Lung is the imperial dragon, his five claws chasing the precious pearl.

The Magic of the Nine Dragon Sons

The true dragon has nine sons, each of whom has a different appearance and possesses different attributes and powers. Described in some of the older Chinese classics, few people today are familiar with them. These sons of dragons traditionally appeared on bells, temple rooftops, palaces, and swords and express the nine distinct applications of the dragon image as a kind of amulet.

Engraved on goblets and wine glasses, the dragon symbol brings plenty to drink, on medicine bottles it invokes the healing powers of the dragon sons. If used to decorate the covers of books and literary works the dragon brings knowledge and scholarship. When the dragon image is carved on door handles it brings precious yang energy to main entrance doors thereby enhancing the luck of good directions. And finally, if you display the symbol of the dragon carp – the fish that jumps across the dragon gate, or *lung men*, to become a scholar, thereby transforming into a dragon – you will attract the powerful chi of scholastic success. Many Chinese people believe that if you place the image of the dragon carp above your main door, it is said that as you cross the threshold each morning and go off to work you will have successfully become a dragon!

Pu Lao, the first dragon son, acts as a protector. Carved on bells and gongs to warn of danger, he ensures security, safety, and protection from all your enemies.

Chu Niu, the second son, is carved onto musical instruments and brings musical excellence. Having a dragon carved on to your musical instrument will ensure some measure of fame in a musical profession.

Suanni, the third son, is embroidered on robes and jackets. He brings a life of comfort, luxury, and great wealth. Look for robes and coats that have the dragon image embroidered in gold and silver thread and you too could live like an emperor! I have just such a jacket and the dragons imbue the jacket with a very special energy. Every time I wear it I feel like an empress indeed!

Yaitzu, the fourth son, is carved on sword hilts at the point where the blade is fitted onto the handle. Yaitzu goes bravely forth into battle and is the inspiration of many an aspiring warrior. If you want the luck of a hero and the courage of a soldier, carry a dragon sword.

Chih Wen, the fifth son, adorns bridges, temple tops, and the roofs of large mansions to protect the household from fire. If you live near a volcano or in a place that is susceptible to fire, placing a dragon image on your rooftop will ensure protection for the household.

Chaofeng, the sixth dragon son, is also carved onto rooftops and on the eaves of temples. He possesses the power to overcome the negative powers of evil and wandering spirits, thereby protecting the home and ensuring that none of these spirits can gain entrance. Placing this dragon above the door or on the rooftop of your home will create the essence of both the fifth and sixth sons.

Pihsi, the seventh dragon son, is the one with supernatural powers. This is a dragon possessing enormous strength and a fantastic knowledge of literature. He is carved onto stone tablets and pedestals. If you want the luck of the scholar and the wisdom of the sages, place a pair of tablets carved with a dragon's image inside your home to simulate the spirit and prodigious power of Pihsi.

Pahsia, the eighth dragon son, is carved at the base of great monuments. This ensures that the monument will never fall, because this is the dragon

that ensures a good foundation. If you, too, place a dragon image at the bottom of your foundations, you will create the chi essence of this powerful dragon, ensuring a sturdy home.

Pikan, the ninth son, is a scaly, one-horned dragon that resembles the Pi Yao – the best creature to pacify the Grand Duke Jupiter, the God of the year who can cause havoc if disturbed (see page 166). Pikan also has the power to overcome the Grand Duke Jupiter. So if you choose to wear this dragon's image or use it in your home you can safely sit facing the Grand Duke, even though this usually results in bad luck and misfortune. Remember if you do so that you must use an image of a dragon with one horn only, or you will not have successfully evoked the spirit of Pikan.

The Pi Yao, also known as Pi Kan, helps appease the bad influence of the Grand Duke Jupiter.

dragon rituals
ensure travel protection

You can use powerful element magic to protect yourself against all manner of bad luck when you are about to embark on a journey. The rituals encompass the use of dragon fire energy, water energy, metal energy, earth energy, and wood energy, and require you to perform some simple acts, which take only a few minutes, just before you are about to set out on your journey.

The observance of these rituals ensures that if you happen to be starting out at an inauspicious time, on an inauspicious date, or if the karma of that journey brings you obstructions, inconveniences, and bad business judgment, you will be guarded against any manifestations of bad Feng Shui. At the least these rituals guard against robbery, lost luggage, and missed connections. At their shining best, these rituals could save you from mortal danger.

When traveling toward the southwest or northeast, swipe the air with a cut branch three or four times in the direction of travel.

First, decide in which direction you will be traveling. Take this direction to mean from point A, your embarkation city, to point B, your destination city. Do the appropriate ritual just before leaving the house to set off on your journey.

- When you are traveling west or northwest, use a dragon incense holder and burn some joss sticks to create smoke, and then, as the smoke rises, use three red candles, and swipe the air in a wide broad curve nine times. The candles should remain lit. If the candles go out do it again until you are able to make three clean sweeps in the direction you are traveling to – west or northwest.

- Dragon water energy is required when you are traveling south. Look for a pail or a water goblet that has a dragon image on it. Just before leaving the house fill the goblet full of water and then, facing south, sprinkle water with your right hand once in a southerly direction.

- Dragon metal energy is required when you are traveling east or southeast. Look for a small curved knife, preferably one with the dragon image on its handle. The knife need not be very big but it should be made of metal and, if it is made of seven types of metal, so much the better. Just before leaving the house, stand facing east or southeast (depending on your travel direction) and, extending your arms wide, use the knife to swipe the air in the direction to which you are traveling six or seven times.

- Dragon earth energy is required when you are traveling in a northerly direction. Use a porcelain bowl decorated with a dragon for this. Place some earth inside the bowl and standing to face the direction you are going, sprinkle the earth eight times in that direction.

- Dragon wood energy is required when you are traveling to the southwest or northeast. Use a freshly cut branch with leaves, and then swipe the air three or four times in the direction of your destination.

sky hangings
send messages to the cosmos

Message banners are powerful affirmations of prosperity at Chinese New Year. Hung close to a door or window, they welcome abundance into your home.

Like the wish balloons, the Chinese believe that sky hangings can send your messages into the cosmos, there to be read and acted upon by the powerful sky dragons that are in reality messengers to the gods and deities who reside in the pure Land of Paradise Mountains. The ritual requires you to hang these banners displaying auspicious words like "Let my wealth arrive," or "May five types of good fortune visit this household" high above your home. The Chinese do this every new year when they place powerful wealth and prosperity affirmations near their doorways to attract good luck in the year ahead.

There are no limits to your creativity here. You can make long banners that flutter in the breeze or you can make hundreds of little flag messages, which you can string up and hang across the front of your house like bunting. You can use some of the traditional Chinese messages – the message "Our wealth has arrived" or "Blessings on this home" are other powerful phrases. Alternatively, you can make up your own auspicious words or phrases. You can use any phrase in any language that you are comfortable with. You can stick your messages around the walls of your home during the New Year or place them on signboards, or hang them up as wealth flags or auspicious banners above your front door.

If you decide to string up your messages, just be sure that you hang your banners up high so that the wind catches them for the wind contains all the chi, both positive and negative, in our environment. Each time the wind blows the messages get strengthened and your wish gets absorbed into the cosmic chi. Be careful to hang your banner in a gentle wind, which carries the benevolent sheng chi, or as the Chinese so lyrically describe it, the dragon's cosmic breath. If the wind is too powerful, it is overwhelming and may contain killing energy that destroys your wishes.

The Fook symbol is a bringer of good fortune. Many Chinese restaurants display it to keep their profits rolling in.

The Chinese have many auspicious words and prosperity phrases that they know off by heart. These magical words that invoke money luck, abundance, and prosperity are almost second nature to them. Thus the word "fook," for instance, which means luck, is universally recognized and acknowledged as an auspicious word which has the power to attract great good fortune to you and your household.

water dragons
bring money luck

There is good water flow and bad water flow, and these reflect the yin and yang chi of the powerful water dragon. To build a water dragon in the home is to attract fabulous good wealth luck yet it is also fraught with danger and risks as it is easy to get the application wrong. However, if you follow the ritual offered here you will find it is an extremely simple and easy way of making sure the flow of water around your home is auspicious.

Do not mistake a body of water as being a water flow. A flow of water implies that the water should move in a certain direction. The more complex water dragon formula specifies the inward flow and the outward flow – the entry and exit of water to and from your property. The simple water dragon flow specifies only that the direction of water as it moves past your main front door should be correct.

To determine the correct direction – that is whether the water should be flowing left to right or right to left – depends on the direction the front

When your main door is facing a cardinal direction, in other words, north, south, east, or west, the water should flow past the main front door from left to right. This means that when you are standing inside the home looking out, the water should be moving from left to right.

When the main door is facing a secondary direction, in other words, northeast, northwest, southeast, or southwest, the water should flow past the main front door from right to left. This means, once again, that if you are standing in the house looking outward the water is moving from right to left.

door faces. For the purposes of this formula, your front door is regarded as the door most often used by the home's inhabitants.

This means you must stand at the doorway and look out and from there, take the compass direction. Use a good-quality compass, such as a surveyor's compass, in order to measure this direction. Try to ensure as much accuracy as you can.

A flow of water implies that you should either construct a small feature like a brook or small stream, or you can use the drain to create the water flow. What you actually can do is determined by the size of your plot of land and also the demands of your budget. The formula given on the following pages gives you the exit directions that are good and bad.

Use a compass to determine your main door direction to see if the flow of water past your home is auspicious.

The Exit Direction

The main thing to take note of is the exit direction of the water from your land. It is extremely crucial that you get this exit direction correct. After the water has flowed past your main front door, if it flows out of the land in the wrong direction, your money drains out. But if it flows out of the land in the correct direction, your wealth multiplies. The exit direction of the water flow depends on the facing direction of your main front door. This is divided into twelve different categories.

Auspicious water exit directions

Main Door Facing	Best Exit Direction	Good Exit Direction
S1 and S2 (ping wu)	W3, NW1 (sin shih) 3 precious jewels	S3, SW1 (ting wei) Wealth & longevity, power
S3 and SW1 (ting wei)	SE2, SE3 (shun Tze) Spectacular wealth & success	SW2, SW3 (kun sen) 10,000 cases of money
SW2 and SW3 (kun sen)	E3, SE1 (yi shen) Golden City direction	S3, SW1 (ting wei) Power and wealth
W1 and W2 (ken yu)	N3, NE1 (kway choh) Money flows in non-stop	W3, NW1 (sin shih) Wealth & success
W3 and NW1 (sin shih)	SW2, SW3 (kun sen) Immense prosperity	NW2, NW3 (chien hai) 10,000 cases of money
NW2 and NW3 (chien hai)	S3, SW1 (ting wei) Wealth for 5 generations	W3, NW1 (sin shih) Excellent sons & wealth
N1 and N2 (zen cher)	E3, SE1 (yi shen) Enormous wealth	N3, NE1 (kway choh) Prosperity for husband & wife
N3 and NE1 (kway choh)	NW2, NW3 (chien hai) Every kind of success	NE2, NE3 (gen yin) Family wealth expands
NE2 and NE3 (gen yin)	W3, NW1 (sin shih) Golden pathway direction	N3, NE1 (kway choh) Money & success luck
E1 and E2 (chia mau)	S3, SW1 (ting wei) Triple jewels luck	E3, SE1 (yi shen) Great wealth & honors
E3 and SE1 (yi shen)	NE2, NE3 (gen yin) Triple jewels luck	SE2, SE3 (shun Tze) Big money flows in
SE2 and SE3 (shun Tze)	N3, NE1 (kway choh) Excellent descendants	E3, SE1 (yi shen) Children benefits

Dangerous water exit directions

Main Door Facing	Bad Exit Direction	Worst Exit Direction
S1 and S2 (ping wu)	N3, NE1 (kway choh) Misfortunes to children	SE2, SE3 (shun Tze) Death path; loss of wealth
S3 and SW1 (ting wei)	NE2, NE3 (gen yin) Wealth dissipates. Son suffers	N3, NE1 (kway choh) Severe loss of money and illness
SW2 and SW3 (kun sen)	NE2, NE3 (gen yin) Sorrow and unhappiness	N3, NE1 (kway choh) Enormous bad luck
W1 and W2 (ken yu)	SW3, W1 (sen ken) Total loss & disaster	S3, SW1 (ting wei) Loss of wealth & descendants
W3 and NW1 (sin shih)	SE2, SE3 (shun Tze) Loss of money, ill health	E3, SE1 (yi shen) Total disaster & calamity
NW2 and NW3 (chien hai)	SE2, SE3 (shun Tze) Disastrous from the start	SW2, SW3 (kun sen) Long life of poverty
N1 and N2 (zen cher)	S3, SW1 (ting wei) No descendants luck	NW2, NW3 (chien hai) Death path
N3 and NE1 (kway choh)	S3, SW1 (ting wei) Poverty & misfortunes	E3, SE1 (yi shen) Failures & Disappointments
NE2 and NE3 (gen yin)	NW2, NW3 (chien hai) Failures & misfortunes	SW2, SW3 (kun sen) Extreme bad luck
E1 and E2 (chia mau)	N3, NE1 (kway choh) Bad luck for women & children	S1, S2 (ping wu) the Death path direction
E3 and SE1 (yi shen)	W1, W2 (ken yu) Difficulties, problems	W3, NW1 (sin shih) Misfortunes & bad luck
SE2 and SE3 (shun Tze)	E1, E2 (chia mau) Bad luck gets worse	NW2, NW3 (chien hai) Death path. Misfortunes

Once you know which category your main door faces then you can refer to the classic Water Dragon formula and choose from all the variations of water flows, exits, and so forth. What is being given here is a very simplified, but extremely powerful, distillation of this formula. I have extracted and simplified this formula here so that this is all you need to be aware of.

Given in this table are the twelve categories of houses based on the directions the door faces and the two good exit directions that bring wealth, as well as the two bad exit directions, which must be avoided at all costs – or your prosperity will dwindle rather than multiply.

My old friends in Chinese banking circles used to tell me that wealth luck was the easiest to activate successfully when using Feng Shui. There are simply so many different ways to enhance prosperity luck – usually with a good degree of success. The extent to which your wealth increases after using Feng Shui will depend on other dimensions of your luck. Not everyone has the karma to become as wealthy as Bill Gates, but Feng Shui can bring you a more comfortable life and a better standard of living if you activate some of the rituals of wealth contained in these pages. This, together with the practice of protective Feng Shui, will ensure that you will always be more than comfortable.

two

prosperity rituals to create wealth

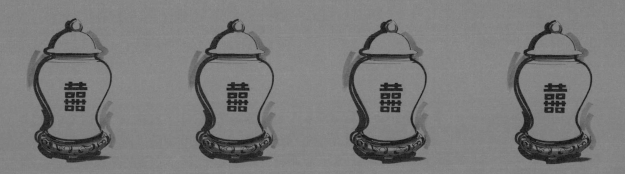

selecting abundance fish
to double your income

Fish have always been highly revered by the Chinese, not just because the Chinese word *yu* means both fish and abundance, but also because their reproductive powers make them a symbol of fertility. And because they swim happily in their own environment, fish have become an emblem of connubial bliss and harmony as well.

To use the fish symbol successfully you can either keep live fish in an aquarium or a pond, or you can eat fish during festive occasions like the lunar New Year. The Chinese do not seem to discriminate between whether the fish should be kept or eaten, unless of course they are practicing Buddhists and therefore vegetarian. Personally, I have stopped eating what the Chinese refer to as swimming fish – fish kept alive in restaurants so they are guaranteed to be cooked fresh. I was advised by my Buddhist friends that each time any creature is slaughtered specifically to make a dish and it is accepted and eaten, the karma of killing that creature will rebound on the person who has consumed it. Instead, I have decided that keeping live fish or the image of the fish is the best way of activating abundance luck. More importantly, the daily act of feeding fish creates good karma, and therefore even more abundance.

Almost all varieties of auspiciously colored fish can be good Feng Shui, but this depends on their temperament and living habits. However, there are specific guidelines regarding keeping fish in aquariums or displaying the fish image in the home in order to create prosperity luck.

The first secret is the variety and number of fish to be kept in an aquarium, and the second has to do with exactly which part of the home represents the best place for fish. As with other auspicious creatures, it is necessary to energize the correct sector and avoid activating harmful corner chi inadvertently.

The Aquarium

Make sure your aquarium is the right size. Balance is vital; if it is too small, it might not be as effective, and if it is too large, the excess of water in a small room could cause problems. Too much water symbolically drowns you. Always keep the water well oxygenated and clean since this generates precious yang energy that

Fish are a potent wealth-bringers. Choose nine fish, because the number nine indicates heaven on earth, and make sure one fish is black, to symbolically absorb any negative energy.

will ensure your fish stay healthy. If any of your fish die for no apparent reason, replace them with new ones and give all the remaining fish a bath of appropriate medicine. Do not worry about a fish dying, but say a silent prayer for its departed soul. Fish that die are believed to have helped you avoid some specific misfortune. But for first-timers, fish may die because they may not have adjusted to the Ph level of the water. Sometimes when you add new fish to an aquarium the old fish will suddenly die unless you also change at least half the water inside the aquarium. However, if fish that have previously been happy and healthy suddenly start to die for no reason it is a warning that some misfortune is about to befall you that has been reduced by the presence of the fish.

The Number of Fish

The number nine represents the fullness of heaven and earth. You should therefore keep eight red, gold, or silver and red fish together with a single black fish. This combination of eight yang-colored fish with one yin-colored fish will ensure not just prosperity but also protection against loss and treachery. If you wish to keep more than nine goldfish, you should keep them in multiples of nine. However, if you are intending to keep an arrowana, a single arrowana in the north sector is the most potent. If you want to keep more than one, five is a good number.

The Arrowana or Dragon Fish

In recent years the tropical arrowana or dragon fish has become increasingly popular as a powerful Feng Shui energizer of wealth luck, but is also used extensively as a symbol of protection. The shape and color of these exceptionally beautiful fish vary according to where they originate. Those wishing to keep arrowana should be careful – it is only those varieties whose scales show a tinge of pink, gold, or silver that are prized specimens for Feng Shui purposes. These fish are extremely expensive, both to buy and to maintain, since they generally prefer to feed on live fish, prawns, and worms. However, I do urge you to try to teach your arrowana to feed on fish pellets, as I did, since feeding them live bait is really bad for your karma.

The Goldfish

The Chinese word *kum yu* means both goldfish and gold in abundance. For this reason the deep red goldfish is the all-time favorite symbol for excellent wealth Feng Shui. To use the goldfish to enhance your wealth

Feng Shui, it is a good idea to go for the varieties that look fat and prosperous and are red or gold in color. Thus the specially developed Japanese ryukins, which are a bright red, are an excellent choice. The lion-headed Chinese varieties that have white silver scales and a bright red head are also excellent. When you choose your black goldfish, make sure that it swims vigorously and is completely black with no other markings.

Keep your goldfish in an aquarium, or in a goldfish bowl with a filter to ensure the water stays clean and oxygenators to keep the water energized with Yang energy. It is particularly beneficial to place your aquarium at floor level so that you look down at the fish from above. Place this auspicious water feature in the north part of your garden or living room for maximum good luck, or place it in the east or southeast. Never place live goldfish in water in the south part of your home. In the south, goldfish can sometimes do more harm than good.

Please remember that you should never mix your fish species; they simply cannot coexist. Fish can be extremely cannibalistic of other varieties!

Arrowana fish are good Feng Shui because they energize your wealth luck.

In Chinese legend, the carp swims upstream and over the mythical "dragon gate" to transform into an awesome dragon. Displaying the dragon carp in your home attracts academic success.

The Carp

The story of the sturgeons of the Yellow River valiantly swimming against the current to reach and jump over the Dragon Gate (*lung men*) during the third moon of each year, thereby turning into celestial dragons, has become the legend of the dragon carp. It has made the carp a symbol of perseverance and martial, literary, and scholastic success. From this legend certain rituals evolved which, over time, have come to be part of the traditions observed by the noble families of China.

The carp seldom fails to deliver. So if you wish your children to excel in their examinations and go on to carve magnificent careers for themselves, keep lots of carp in a pond inside or outside the house. If you intend to keep fish outside, then you must ensure that they are protected from predators. There is also a strict taboo that Feng Shui masters stress time and time again, and that is if you have a pond outside the house you must be sure that it is on the left hand side of the front door, rather than the right. If the pond is on the right rather than the left, wealth may ensue but it will also bring a breakdown in relationships within the household.

Alternatively, and perhaps even more effective, is to find an image of the dragon carp. If you visit Hong Kong, China, or your local Chinatown, look out for a pair of dragon carp fashioned out of wood, porcelain, or brass and place them high above the entrance doorway into your home. The material they are made of should reflect the element of the facing direction of the door. So doors facing east, south, and southeast would benefit from wood images; doors facing northeast or southwest would benefit from porcelain images; while those facing west, north, and northwest would benefit from metallic images. The presence of the dragon carp above the doorway indicates that each time you step out of the home you become a dragon, full of strength, determination, and courage. As if by magic, you will feel yourself taking on the attributes of the mighty dragon.

The dragon carp image is especially excellent for those hoping to rise up the corporate career ladder, those in the political field seeking election or promotion, and those in the military. The dragon carp image is probably one of the best gifts you can possibly give to an aspiring politician, civil servant, or anyone set on a career where upward mobility depends on attracting power luck.

The double fish is an ancient symbol of sexual union and successful partnerships.

The Double Fish Symbol

In ancient China, fish were almost always included as one of the items in the betrothal gifts given to the parents of the bride. A pair of fish was symbolic of the joys of union, particularly of a sexual nature and the fish emblem was also believed to be a charm against bad luck since it is included among the auspicious signs on the footprints of the Buddha.

The double fish symbol is regarded as one of the eight treasures and is usually embroidered on to door curtains and pillowcases for good luck. The double fish symbol is both a protective amulet and an enhancer of good chi, Sheng Chi, worn to attract good luck. In Thailand, children are often given the double fish symbol to wear around their necks. These are usually made of gold, and sometimes set with precious stones like rubies, sapphires, and emeralds.

I have discovered that if the double fish symbol is present when the family is together, it ensures that the family stays together harmoniously. The phrase "staying together" has many implications – it means that no harm will come to any member of the family, no outsider will entice a member of the family away, there are good relations between the generations and between siblings and, most important of all, the husband and wife will not do anything to jeopardize the unity of the family. Divorces and separations will thus be reduced.

The best way to introduce this is in the dining area where the family sits down together for a meal. In the past, double fish symbols were carved onto dining tables. In my own home I have designed a glass-topped turntable very similar to the "lazy susan" used in many Chinese restaurants. I have the double fish symbol etched onto the glass top and it has served my family and me very well.

making
wealth waterfalls

One of the most powerful wealth rituals is the correct construction of the wealth-bringing waterfall. There are several ways to approach this particular prosperity ritual. It can be as simple as a tiny simulated flow of water in a small porcelain bowl – the Taiwanese have come up with a few ready-made waterfalls – or it can be a massive artificial waterfall. The key is to correctly identify the part of a property where the placement of a waterfall would benefit the fortunes of the house or apartment building.

To be effective in creating fast and substantial wealth luck, prosperity waterfalls should neither be too steep nor too gentle so that the strength of the water falling is neither too slow, so that it looks like only a trickle of water, nor too fast so it rushes past.

Most importantly, waterfalls should be positioned so that the water never appears to flow away from the home but should seem to be flowing towards the home from an auspicious direction. If there is a small pond where water can collect and settle, then prosperity is said to accumulate.

There should always be a door to symbolically receive the flow of wealth-bringing water. Even if the main door is somewhere else, you can open another door to let the waterfall's auspicious chi enter the home.

The most auspicious waterfall is one that seems to enter into the dining room of the home since this feeds directly into the belly of the home. So if you find it auspicious to build a waterfall directly outside you dining room then a prosperity pond of water has the potential to bring enormous wealth opportunities.

If you have no door through which you can receive the wealth-giving chi, then windows are the next-best thing. Remember, if you go to the trouble of building an artificial waterfall it is a good idea to do everything possible to capture the chi created. So if you cannot open a door, open a window. However, if you live in a high-rise apartment you should not attempt to build a prosperity waterfall, as this will create bad luck for those living below you.

Placed correctly the waterfall brings absolutely fabulous wealth luck, but if your karma is not ready, you will encounter all kinds of impediments. You might make all sorts of excuses as to why you cannot proceed or construction may prove difficult. But if it is your time to prosper you will discover that building this waterfall is quite simply effortless and well worthwhile.

A waterfall generates wealth when it cascades towards the house, bringing abundance to, rather than from, the home. When situated close to a dining room, the luck of abundance is said to come into the belly of the home, symbolically feeding the residents.

Creating Your Own Waterfall

If you want to build a waterfall in the garden to create prosperity magic, here are some guidelines to bear in mind:

🖌 The best compass sector to build a prosperity waterfall is the sector in the garden which corresponds to the place where the water star 8 is located. Please refer to Chapter six to locate the exact sector in your garden that would benefit most from such a waterfall.

🖌 If for some reason you are unable to determine the place of the water star 8 in your garden, then you should build a waterfall only in the north, the east, the southeast, or the southwest corners of the land. When you investigate the land around your home, select one of these four directions

Waterfalls built in the southwest should have two tiers. Place a dragon statuette for wealth luck. If you have terrapins, they will also bring you good fortune.

that seems the most practical in terms of the layout of your home. If none of these four sectors of your land is conducive to building a waterfall, then it is safer not to do so. Judge the suitability of the sectors according to the general contours of the land as well as whether the falling water can be symbolically received into a suitable part of the home. If the water flows toward a toilet it will be an exercise in futility, and should be avoided at all costs.

❧ Waterfalls that are built in the east should have three levels of falling water. Those built in the southeast should have four levels of falling water. Those in the north should have either six or seven levels of falling water, and waterfalls built in the southwest sectors should have two tiers of falling water.

❧ Try to build a filtration system where the pump can be located. This is the surest way of keeping the water clean and auspicious. It is also a good idea to keep fish and plants that help to keep the water clean.

❧ If the waterfall is in the north, it is an excellent idea to keep some live tortoises if you are able. This will be most auspicious. If it is in the east or southeast, keep live fish – carp or arrowana are best. And if the waterfall is in the southwest, simply grow water lilies or lotuses. All of these measures will bring wonderful yang energy to your waterfall.

Fish are a wonderful energizer for waterfalls located in the southeast of the garden.

❧ Always keep an image of a dragon near the waterfall. If the waterfall is in the north the dragon should be made of brass; in the east or southeast, a wooden dragon would be great; and in the southwest, a porcelain dragon is the best. If it is difficult to get these specified dragons then placing an image made of any of these materials is better than not placing a dragon. It is the placement of a dragon that will make the waterfall more effective in attracting wealth luck.

Tibetan Buddhist Wealth Jambhalas

The Tibetan Buddhists have wealth deities who are believed to manifest in order to help those in need of money. These wealth deities, or Jambhalas, are believed to be most effective in bringing wealth to the home when they are properly placed under falling water.

There are altogether five different Jambhalas:

The green Jambhala, usually shown with its consort

The yellow Jambhala, usually depicted seated

The black Jambhala, usually shown standing

The white Jambhala, usually shown seated on a dragon

The red Jambhala, usually shown resembling the Hindu God Ganesh, with an elephant countenance.

The Buddhist Jambhalas usually have stern expressions on their faces, and they are always holding a mongoose from whose mouth spews forth precious gems, gold, and other manifestations of wealth. At the foot of the Jambhala should be placed a pile of such manifestations of wealth.

The ritual for enticing the Jambhala to make its mongoose spew forth jewels and gold is to create a continuous stream of water falling directly onto the crown of its head. This ritual, plus the regular chanting of prayers and mantras to the Jambhalas, will attract auspicious wealth luck to your home.

Each of the five Jambhalas has a different mantra and *sadhana* (spiritual visualization). To do the Jambhala practice with full mantra chanting and offerings, it is best to seek out the help of a qualified lama who has the correct lineage, and to then very respectfully request an initiation. An initiation is like asking for blessings and permission to do the Jambhala practice, and then it will be most powerful.

Those who wish may, however, look for and display the Jambhalas as described on their prosperity waterfalls. You can find Jambhala statues at any Tibetan or Nepali shop that sells Buddhist images and holy objects.

If you create your Jambhala wealth waterfall with the correct respectful attitude not only will your wish for prosperity materialize but, far more importantly, it will actually create the opportunity for you to meet with a holy lama. If you meet such a teacher and guide then you will discover that the spiritual benefits you receive will far outweigh any material riches that may come your way. Remember, when you practice this ritual that you should always do so with respect and humility.

The yellow Jambhala is a Tibetan wealth deity that is placed under falling water to bring money to those in need.

prosperity coins
stimulate instant wealth chi

For business success, tie three or six Chinese coins to the front of a file or invoice book. Tying them with red cord or ribbon activates the coins with potent yang energy.

Coins are wonderful prosperity symbols. When placed on invoice books, in your handbag, on work files, or pasted on telephones, fax machines, and computers, and activated with red or gold threads, ribbons, and ropes, they can be used to magnify prosperity luck. These colored ribbons activate yang energy and, when they are skillfully tied together in auspicious numbers and with special-meaning knots, the results can be rather spectacular. There are several different ways to combine knots and coins to bring out the chi hidden within the coins.

Old Chinese coins or modern reproductions are extremely popular with Feng Shui practitioners familiar with their powerful significance. This is because when used correctly they can be extremely potent in calling upon the luck of both heaven

and earth. The square holes in the center of the round coins symbolize the fusion of heaven and earth, bringing prosperity chi, which is believed to activate and energize prosperity luck.

The Ten Emperor Coins

A very popular Feng Shui feature to hang in the office are coins taken from each of the ten Emperors' reigns tied together with red thread or gold ribbon – especially when tied with the mysterious never-ending knot. They should be placed strategically, either behind where you sit or on your left side to simulate the dragon. This Feng Shui enhancer is a symbol of wealth since it represents the prosperity of ten dynasties, hence its name. The coins used can be either genuine antique coins from ten different Emperor's reigns, or they can be copies of these coins. In Feng Shui it does not seem to really matter if you use fake or real coins.

However, there are those who believe that genuine antique coins carry the chi of their period of origin. If you are so fortunate as to come in to possession of original coins from an auspicious reign, wrap these coins in soft yellow silk cloth and sleep with them under your pillow. If possible sew them onto the mattress so they do not move about to ensure that your prosperity will be never-ending, even from this life to the next. Even if you only have coins from one reign, they would be most auspicious if that reign period was successful and prosperous. Coins from the Chien Lung Empire would be regarded as auspicious period coins.

Hiding Coins in Walls and Floors

The most fantastic way to use coins to seriously enhance your Feng Shui is to get a few hundred coins, tie them up in groups of three or six using red thread or gold ribbon, and then arrange with a building contractor to lay them in the ground or pathway leading to your home, as well as in the walls of your living and dining room. This means that the coins get plastered into the walls and cemented onto your floors. The significance of undertaking this major exercise is to symbolically bring wealth into your home and it will lead to a steady increase in your standard of living.

Coins are most beneficial when they are placed in the west, north, and northwest sectors of the home so that if the front of your house faces any one of these directions, then the hidden coins will energize wealth luck. This is a ritual to remember if you happen to be building or renovating your home.

If any of your relatives or loved ones are building a home at this moment, you should share this wealth-enhancing ritual with them. Obviously this particular ritual is suitable only for those of you who are living in your own homes. There is not much point in going to the expense of doing this in rented premises.

Other types of coins can also be used to enrich the chi of your household. Try to find large, heavy brass or gold-plated coins that have auspicious words on one side of the coin and the trigrams arranged in an Early Heaven arrangement on the other side. Such coins take on protective attributes and can be used on curtain tiebacks.

More significantly these coins are also very effective as Feng Shui metal cures to overcome the deadly Five Yellow star number wherever it flies each year. In 2003, the Five Yellow is in the southeast sector, thus

In 2003, the misfortune star, the Five Yellow flies to the southeast. If your bedroom falls in this sector, counteract the Five Yellow by tying three Chinese coins to each curtain tieback.

placing six of these powerful coins in the southeast will very effectively protect residents from the deadly effects of the Five Yellow.

This becomes extremely vital when your front door or bedroom is located in the sector afflicted. If it is your main door that is being negatively affected by the Five Yellow, place six of these special coins under the doormat coming into the house.

If it is in the bedroom, then stringing three coins on each half of the curtain drapes, making a total of six coins, should be an effective countermeasure against the Five Yellow.

Tying nine Chinese coins around a wealth deity, such as Fuk, for a set period of time empowers the coins with the virtue of that deity. The coins are then considered to be an amulet of protection for children.

Coin Amulets to Protect Children From the "Thirty Danger Barriers"

In addition to bringing prosperity, good fortune coins can also be used as protective and auspicious amulets that are considered to be most beneficial for children. Nine coins taken from the Chien Lung period (either the genuine old coins or gold/jade imitations will be acceptable) should be tied with red string and hung around the neck of a deity of wealth for 7, 14, or 21 days. This would symbolically empower the coins with the deity's chi and thus acquire virtue.

The coins should then be worn around the neck of the child to overcome the 30 dangerous barriers of a person's life. The number of coins to be hung around the neck would be equal to how old the child is (in the

Chinese statement of age please add one year); and each year a fresh coin would be added during the first day of the lunar new year until the child attains the age of 15. By that time the child is believed to have symbolically and successfully crossed all the barriers along the path of life.

These barriers are the four seasons, the four pillars, the demon cow king, the devil's gate demon, the insurmountable difficulties, the golden hen falling into a well, and the barrier of the private parts. Then there are the barriers of the hundred days, the broken bridge, the nimble foot, the five genii, the golden padlock, the iron snake, the bathing tub, the white tiger, and the Buddhist monks.

Then there are the barriers posed by the heavenly dog; that invoking heaven's pity; and those associated with the lock and with the key; where the bowels are sundered; and where the head is broken. This creates the barriers of the thousand days; of the nocturnal weeping; of the burning broth; of the time when children are buried; and where life is shortened, caused by the general's dagger, deep running water, or caused by fire and water – all colorful stuff. Basically, what this means is that the coin amulets overcome all the dangers of growing up!

Coin amulets are used to protect children against the Thirty Danger Barriers – or the trials of growing up. The number of coins a child wears signifies their age.

Swords of Coins

Over time the use of these coin amulets became something of a superstition, and the coins worn around the neck evolved into clusters of coins tied to resemble swords, decorated with knots and tassels. These sword coins are now used for warding off shar chi or killing breath and are known as *Pi Hsieh Chien*.

These knife coins, whose origin goes right back to the 1st century BCE, are believed to make excellent antidotes for Feng Shui afflicted corners, which threaten the loss of the family's wealth. You can place these knife coins in the corners of your home that give you problems, although they are really believed to be most effective for overcoming losses in commercial life.

Always hang the sword coins on the northwest or west walls of the office behind you. This symbol should never be hung in front of you, since this turns the potency of the sword against you.

It is not vital, as with other symbols, to display the sword of coins at a particular time. However, if you want optimum results and to display the sword coins to real effect, bring them out on a metal day at a metal hour. If you have one readily available, you should therefore check your Chinese Almanac accordingly to verify which day and hour to choose.

If you are not in a corporate or political environment, my advice is to ignore the sword of coins – you do not need its aggressive chi to overcome the kind of bad luck encountered in domestic life. It is only when you have to contend with the often ruthless nature of commerce or politics that the sword of coins becomes an invaluable Feng Shui tool.

Coin swords are a potent antidote to corporate back-stabbing. Display one behind you in the office to ward off enemies!

Coins to Enhance the Wealth of a Marriage

In the Imperial Record of Chinese Coins, it was recorded that there is a certain form of coin-shaped talisman known as "coins for throwing into the bed chamber" which would not only bring great wealth to the couple but also plenty of successful children. The story goes that one of the Emperors of the Tang Dynasty had coins fashioned of gold and silver, and engraved with various auspicious phrases, thrown onto the marriage bed of his favorite daughter on the advice of his Feng Shui adviser. Thus coins were used not only to attract riches, but also to ward off killing energy and to ensure the dynastic continuance of a family. To strengthen the luck of young married couples you can therefore take a leaf out of these Imperial records and do the same.

Chinese Emperors ritually threw coins onto a daughter's marriage bed to protect future dynasties. A contemporary way to invoke marriage success is to tie coins to the bedpost.

The Money or Coin Tree

There is an old Chinese legend that refers to a money tree with gold coins on its branches. When you shake this money tree, gold coins fall like rain as if from heaven into your garden. This rainfall of coins has become a popular motif in old paintings and on screens, and is a great favorite with Feng Shui enthusiasts who believe in the power of symbolic Feng Shui. Use your creativity to make such a tree. Adorn the branches with lots of old coins and let them hang down auspiciously. Tie the hanging coins together with red thread or gold ribbon. You could also place a dragon amongst the branches to add further symbolism to the tree. Pin auspicious Chinese characters and inscriptions on the stem of the tree and at its base place three red lanterns, which will energize the tree with yang chi.

A Feng Shui gem tree, made from semi-precious stones such as citrine, crystal, or coral, brings awesome money luck. Tie golden coins to the branches to attract benevolent heaven luck.

The expression "shaking the money tree" always means getting rich with little effort. For the wealth tree, coins should be tied into ten strands of one hundred coins. During the lunar New Year red lanterns were hung from the wealth tree to signify wealth all year round.

A variation on the money tree is the gem tree, made entirely of semi-precious stones such as crystals, amethysts, carnelian, citrines, or coral. The stems are usually made of gold. These beautiful trees are extremely auspicious since they create wonderful lucky energy for the whole house. These gem trees are widely available, so you should not have any trouble purchasing one for your home.

I keep my own gem tree, which is made of carnelian, in the northwest side of my living room since this is the corner of chien, thereby signifying wealth from heaven. I also hang gold coins on my gem tree to activate the luck of heaven. You would be well advised to do the same since this little gem tree can bring awesome wealth luck.

invite in the
wealth deities
and get rich

The wealth deity Tsai Shen Yeh is depicted riding a tiger, showing his control over this ferocious creature. Chinese wealth deities are traditionally unsmiling unlike the Laughing Buddha, but here he has been painted smiling to add some mirth to his wealth-bringing potency.

There are wealth deities in many of the eastern traditions. The Koreans and Thais have their wealth Buddhas. The Tibetans have their five Jambhala wealth gods. Chinese Taoists regard the Eight Immortals as beings whose presence in the home either on paintings or on decorative items is believed to be most auspicious. But the most popular and powerful wealth gods are the three star gods also known as Fuk Luk Sau.

Placing these wealth deities in the home, especially directly facing the main door is believed to transform incoming chi into most auspicious energy. There are other auspicious sectors to place wealth gods and when special rituals accompany their entrance into the home, their potency in bringing good wealth luck into the home is seriously enhanced. Familiarize yourself with the Chinese deities of wealth, and then get to know the deity of wealth in your own culture.

Tsai Shen Yeh

The Chinese have several deities that they regard as the wealth god. One of the most popular is Tsai Shen Yeh, who is usually depicted offering an ingot of gold and stepping or sitting on a fierce tiger, to symbolize his control over this animal. In the lunar years of the Tiger, displaying the God of Wealth is particularly auspicious. It is not necessary to pray to this deity, simply invite him into your home as a symbolic gesture.

You can also hang a knotted cluster of nine Chinese coins tied with red thread on this wealth deity since this will very effectively activate the prosperity attributes of the coins.

Fuk Luk Sau

The three star gods, or Fuk Luk Sau, are the deities of health, wealth, and prosperity. These deities can be found in many Chinese homes and they are usually placed in the dining room. Fuk Luk Sau can be fashioned out of brass, or molded from porcelain or cloisonné or carved from sandalwood or ivory. Fuk Luk Sau are said to be exceptionally auspicious and should be invited into the home during an auspicious hour on an auspicious day. If they are brought into the home on the wrong day or hour, their presence does not add very much to the wealth Feng Shui of the home. To check for auspicious days and hours, consult a good authorized translation of the Chinese Almanac.

The best place to display the God of Wealth is on a table, 30 to 33 in (750-800 mm) high, directly facing the main door so that the first thing you see upon entering your home is the wealth god. This placement symbolizes him greeting the chi coming into the home, transforming it into healthy prosperous energy as it flows through the rest of the house.

If this spot is already occupied, you can place the wealth god diagonally opposite the front door, and again, facing toward it. If you have a devotional altar or shrine, do not place your wealth god on it since the wealth god is not a god in the religious sense of the word, but is instead a Taoist deity symbolizing the aspiration of wealth.

Kuan Kung is a powerful protector of businesses, politicians, and other guardians of state. If you display him in your office, he brings support from mentors.

Kuan Kung

Another deity usually regarded as a bringer of wealth is Kuan Kung. In fact, of the many deities of the Chinese pantheon, there is probably none as popular or as colorful as this god of wealth, who is also regarded as the god of war. Among his many other titles, he is the protector of the oppressed, patron saint of police, guardian deity of the triads, and in recent times, protector of politicians and business leaders alike.

Images of Kuan Kung sell like hot cakes. It is believed that when he guards over legitimate businesses he carries his mighty sword in his right hand, and when he is protecting the triads, he carries his sword in his left hand. So when you go looking for the image of Kuan Kung, make certain you observe his sword very carefully and pick the right-handed version as you do not want to give the wrong impression!

The more fierce his countenance, then the more powerful Kuan Kung is said to be. Be careful that you do not lose either his staff or his sword

since these are his weapons, and make sure that they are placed correctly on his image at all times.

There are many different versions of Kuan Kung. His image is usually made of either porcelain or wood and you can find him in any number of different poses. He may be sitting on a horse, sitting on his throne, standing and surveying everyone with a steely gaze, or simply standing in a posture of command. The most powerful Kuan Kung of all is said to be the Nine Dragon Kuan Kung, when he is shown with nine dragons on his body and five dragon flags on his back.

The benefits of inviting Kuan Kung into your office or home include peace and harmony for the residents, awesome protection for the breadwinner, and fantastic prosperity luck for all.

It is believed that leaders and businessmen who place Kuan Kung behind them at work will never lack for powerful support from important people. They will seldom get thwarted or toppled from their positions of authority and power.

> Kuan Kung is most powerful when placed in the northwest corner of a house. He should always face the main door, so that he has his eye on who comes in and out of the home.

There is no necessity to worship Kuan Kung. From a Feng Shui perspective his image is all you need. I have several Kuan Kungs in my house, and continue to be fascinated by the symbolic power of this red-faced general who lived during the times of the warring states.

The Laughing Buddha

Mi Lo Foh, the Laughing Buddha, is probably the most beloved of Buddha images in the pantheon of Chinese deities. He has been referred to as the Buddha of Wealth because his image is believed to attract prosperity and wealth luck to those engaged in any kind of business. Those who consider him the Buddha of Wealth assume that his big satchel symbolizes a bagful of money, gold, and precious gemstones. Some even believe that his sizeable tummy symbolizes wealth so that the bigger the tummy, the more auspicious the image will be.

The Laughing Buddha carries a bag which is thought to contain the troubles of the world; others believe his sack is full of riches. Many Chinese business people believe that stroking his belly brings them good fortune.

To enjoy the Buddha's blessings, they say, you should stroke his big belly each day and so this has become a daily habit of many Chinese businessmen. Many others maintain that the Laughing Buddha is the Buddha of Happiness because nothing gives him greater pleasure than gathering all the world's unhappiness into his bag. This is also the reason for his laughter; that he is able to pick up what he loves most – other people's problems! I love this version of the story of the Laughing Buddha because it seems very authentic and is in accordance with so many other Buddhist teachings.

Many Chinese Buddhists regard the Laughing Buddha as the Buddha who will be revealed in the future – also known as the Maitreya Buddha. This has led to some confusion amongst Buddhists from other countries since all other representations of the Maitreya

Buddha from other cultures depict a handsome, slim, and striking figure. I did some research in order to discover why the Chinese Maitreya, which has become so amazingly popular as an auspicious symbol, looks so fat and oversized, and discovered a most novel explanation. The story goes that Buddha Maitreya in one of his lifetimes was so handsome that many women swooned over him. In his compassion, Maitreya decided to manifest as a fat older man, since this would ensure that he broke no one's heart. Hence the Chinese version of Maitreya is fat and laughing.

In Feng Shui you should place an image of this Buddha in the living room, preferably directly facing the front door and as large as possible. Doing this will be most beneficial to any living space, since auspicious chi is said to emanate from his image. More importantly, a laughing Buddha image also has the power to absorb all the negative or killing chi inside the home, and is an excellent cure for overcoming annual flying stars that bring illness and loss.

If you wish to invest in a Laughing Buddha, select one that is made in a medium which is harmonious with the element of the corner you want to place it in or with the element that is deemed most auspicious for you. You can select any posture you wish, but do take your time selecting one that particularly appeals to you. Anytime you feel dejected, try rubbing his big tummy and look at his face. You will discover that his joy is contagious and his smile will bring a response from somewhere deep within you.

displaying the
five red bats
to attract success

Two bats signify double good fortune. Five bats signify the five blessings of longevity, wealth, health, a life of virtue, and a natural death.

According to a Chinese legend, there are silver-colored bats that live for a thousand years in caverns in the high mountains feeding on stalactites. If you can find them and eat them you will live to a very ripe old age! It is a long-held belief amongst the older generation that any item decorated with the image of the red bat should be regarded with extreme favor, since it symbolizes prosperity, happiness, and longevity. The origin of this positive connotation comes from the sound of its name. In Chinese it is known as the *pian fu* and the word "fu" also sounds like happiness and good fortune. The bat is thus a very popular symbol that is frequently used for decorative purposes. When utilized to enhance Feng Shui, the bat is usually painted in a cinnabar red, because red is the color of joy.

Usually, red bats are drawn in a cluster of five – the pictorial representation of the five blessings from heaven: old age or longevity, wealth, health, love of virtue, and a natural death. Five red bats also represent the yang symbol of prosperity, and they are often found on ceramics and paintings. One of the more auspicious representations is of five bats emerging from a jar or vase. This means not only happiness and good fortune, but also a peaceful life with few problems.

The Chinese believe that if a family of bats take up residence in your home, it is an exceptionally good omen since they offer not only protection, but signify the coming of a time of prosperity and success for the household. Thus bats should never be chased away.

produce an abundance of
yang water

There is a big difference between yin and yang water and it is the knowledge and expertise in differentiating between the two that empowers water practices with great potency. For energizing wealth and success luck, it is necessary to produce an abundance of yang water.

Yang water is water that has life, so that its energy has the power to activate the water element in favor of yang houses. Yang water is usually water in which there are fish, plants, and other manifestations of life; there is also movement and flow. Water can be made yang with a pump or with oxygenators, because both create bubbles and cause water to move with a life force.

Yin water is stagnant, still water. It is water that has been left standing for some time and is usually associated with energy that has gone stale from inertia. Yin water is not necessarily dirty or polluted, but it is quiet water.

In Feng Shui rituals that bring wealth, there should be an abundance of yang energy. Waterfalls are by their very nature made up of yang energy. So make certain that when you wish to activate water for purposes of attracting wealth it is yang water, and not yin water, that you bring into the home.

Prosperous yang water is flowing and fresh, harboring healthy fish and plants.

create
a harbor
for multiple sources of income

A sailing ship for wealth luck should be placed so it faces inward, to bring in money rather than take it away from you. Start by loading it with a cargo of replica gold ingots, then add coins and precious stones to denote wealth.

Since ancient times Chinese merchants have believed in the good-fortune symbol of a merchant sailing ship filled with riches and wealth in the form of precious cargo. Indeed, many Chinese entrepreneurs used the sailing ship as their logo since it symbolized the winds and waters bringing wealth in the guise of more business, more trade, and more turnover.

Next to the dragon, the sailing ship is the most popular symbol used by Chinese businessmen. Just placing these ships inside the home is sufficient to attract great good fortune, especially when the ship has been filled with precious stones, gold, and money.

Creating a harbor within the home is even more powerful, especially when the ships are of the right kind and are placed facing specifically auspicious directions. They should also be positioned correctly and should never be placed high, or pointing outward.

A Sailing Ship Laden with "Gold"

A laden sailing ship is probably one of the best Feng Shui enhancers to have in your office if you want to increase your personal wealth, especially if you are an aspiring entrepreneur or businessman.

Try to find a model merchant ship in full sail that is made of metal (gold is best). Alternatively, wood is also good. If possible, you should get one without any cannons or guns on board and one that has been constructed without a single nail. An additional part of this sailing ship ritual is to place it so it appears as if it is sailing in from your success direction based on your personal KUA number (see page 171). This will ensure that the source of chi for the sailing ship is auspicious for you.

To energize your Feng Shui luck for the office, place a model or replica of a sailing ship near the vicinity of the entrance door. Then make very certain that the sailing ship is sailing inward toward the inside of the office. Do not let the sailing ship face outward, as if it is sailing away. Then fill the sailing ship with as many kinds of precious stones, gold ingots, coins, and real money as you wish. The idea is to suggest a ship loaded with rich and abundant cargo. You can fill the ship with symbolic gold in the form of fake gold ingots, which are readily available. If you cannot find these fake gold ingots, then place coins and money inside the ship instead.

Exactly the same thing can be done for the home. Get a sailing ship and display it near your front door, then position it so that it sails inwards bearing gold and riches. Please note that a ship with sails to "catch the wind" is deemed more auspicious than any other kind of ship, so shop carefully for the right kind of sailing ship.

Also, for this ritual you can use a single sailing ship or many different ships anchored in your home or office to simulate a harbor. Many ships represent many sources of income. If you are able to purchase several ships to place inside your home then each should sail from a direction that signifies success for each member of the family, as this ensures that everyone benefits.

make your own
wealth vase

For many years the ritual of making and consecrating wealth vases to ensure the preservation and continuing growth of the family's wealth remained a closely guarded secret, known only to the élite at court and the highest ranking abbots of temples and monasteries. In recent years, however, with the growing interest in the esoteric rituals of the eastern mystics, different Taoist and Buddhist lineages are now revealing these rituals to the world.

The Laughing Buddha for happiness

Your wealth vase should have a neck, a cover, a fat body, and a solid base, like the blue vase shown in the picture on page 63. Vases that do not have a cover are unsuitable since the vase has to be closed up after it has been filled. If possible get a vase that has an auspicious symbol printed or engraved on it, like the symbol of the double happiness knot.

Your wealth vase can be as large as you wish and as expensive as you can afford. It can be made of porcelain, cloisonné, china, or any pottery. You need only one of these vases yourself, but you can make as many wealth vases as you wish to give to loved ones as gifts.

Three coins for wealth

There are two types of ingredients for your wealth vase: the essential ingredients and the secret ingredients.

The Essential Ingredients of the Wealth Vase

The coin packet for charity

A god of wealth in miniature which can be one of the following: the Laughing Buddha, Tsai Sheng Yeh, Kuan Kung, or any one of the Tibetan gods of wealth. If you can find them, you can place offering goddesses (in

any form you wish) in the vase to attend to the needs of the god of wealth. This is not an essential item but it does help to make your wealth vase more potent.

🏵 Three gold coins tied with red thread or gold ribbon to symbolize wealth in gold. The red thread introduces yang energy, which activates the chi of the coins. When tied in gold thread the wealth signified is multiplied tenfold.

🏵 Nine Chinese coins in a red packet to signify money that will be donated to charity. This further enhances the potency of the wealth vase.

🏵 Ten clear crystals to ensure that your life flows smoothly and there are no obstacles to your pursuit of wealth.

🏵 Ten special lapis lazuli globes – to signify the best of the world's treasures. Lapis lazuli is believed to be the precious material that forms the base of the earth.

🏵 Five pieces of silk or cotton string in the five element colors of white, red, green, blue, and yellow for tying the cover onto the wealth vase. Usually this cotton string is plaited and then used to tie the cotton cloth securely onto the neck of the vase.

🏵 Five square pieces of cotton or silk in the five element colors of white, red, green, blue, and yellow. These square pieces of cloth signify the five elements of the universe.

🏵 Five types of dried foodstuffs wrapped in plastic. Suggested foods are rice, millet, barley, sorghum, and dhal. This symbolizes food for the wealth god.

🏵 If you wish, you can also add seven types of semi precious stones along with an additional 100 coins, and red thread placed deep under the gemstones.

Ten clear crystals to clear obstacles

Ten lapis lazuli globes for treasure

The Secret Ingredients of the Wealth Vase

Earth from a rich man's house, which must be given to you willingly. My advice on how you can get this is to simply ask. The person need not be a millionaire but it should be someone you admire and respect and whose wealth was preferably inherited, in which case the chi of his earth comes from a long line of rich ancestors. If you can get earth from more than one rich man, so much the better. Since you do not need a great deal of earth in a vase, it is a good idea to share your earth with other wealth vases you may make as gifts.

Pictures of six rich men or women. It is easy to get these pictures since those cut from magazines and newspapers are deemed perfectly acceptable.

Money from a rich man's pocket is more difficult to obtain, since you may not steal this money. The best way to do this is to ask a rich person for some loose change. Bring out a large denomination note and change for smaller denominations, and then place one in each wealth vase you are making. Once again, you can ask as many wealthy people for loose change as you wish, since this can only strengthen the wealth chi of your vase.

A picture of a mansion. Select a picture that represents your dream mansion and place this inside the wealth vase to symbolize your personal palace. You can put in more than one mansion if you wish.

Money from nine different countries – if you have traveled widely, this should not be a problem. If not, you can pay a visit to the bank, but you should only include the strong currencies of the world. You should definitely include US dollars, pounds sterling, Deutschmark, and Japanese yen.

Make your wealth vase a vessel for your dreams of riches. Add pictures of six rich people and a mansion, plus some international currencies and a little earth from a rich man's garden.

The Method for Creating a Wealth Vase

🌸 Wipe the vase and, using an aroma stick or incense, symbolically cleanse the wealth vase saying "Om ah hum" three times under your breath. This ensures that the vase has been properly blessed and cleansed. No wandering spirit is then able to make its secret lair within.

🌸 Into the vase, place the nine coins inside a red packet.

🌸 Next add the earth and crystals.

🌸 Now include the food, placed in plastic packets.

🌸 Then put in the wealth god and offering goddesses. Be sure to make a mark on the vase when you are putting the wealth god in to show which way he is facing.

Next, fill the vase with all the secret ingredients.

🌸 Finally, put in the rest of the ingredients.

🌸 By this time the wealth vase will be full so place the lid on it, cover the lid with the cotton squares – first white, then blue, then green, then red, then yellow, so yellow is on top. Then plait the five colored strings and use them to tie the cloth firmly round the lid. This effectively seals in the wealth ingredients.

When the wealth vase has been made it is necessary to consecrate it and this is best done with some incense and aroma sticks. Place the vase inside a cupboard, either in your bedroom or living room, hidden away. Place some food, some water, and some plastic flowers to symbolize offerings to the wealth god inside the cupboard. Make sure that the wealth god is facing inward and not outward so check the mark on your vase. Next, lock the cupboard door securely and do not open it until the lunar New Year when you should replenish the offerings and repeat the whole process.

Never place anything above the cupboard that contains the wealth vase.

Chinese families keep wealth vases that have been passed down from generation to generation. The more carefully you keep these heirlooms the better will the family wealth be preserved. If you so wish, you may make a smaller version filled with even more precious things and keep this one hidden away in a safe.

The ritual I have described is the simplest of the wealth vase rituals. There are other more elaborate rituals, especially those associated with the Tibetan wealth Jambhala Buddhas. These Tibetan wealth vases tend to be a lot rounder and fatter, and the consecration of such wealth vases is accompanied with elaborate pujas and extensive offerings. Usually the wealth Buddha's mantras are recited at least ten thousand times before the wealth vase is consecrated. And the owner of the wealth vase chants the mantra as a daily practice to the wealth Jambhalas.

When you have filled your wealth vase, use incense to consecrate it before placing it in a safe place until the lunar New Year.

Moon magic is largely used to seek help from the god of marriage to send powerful blessings to young couples and aid in their relationships. The origins of this belief come from the realms of folk legends; one is never really certain how much of it is real magic and how much of it comes from the mind. There are very specific symbols which can be placed in certain corners of your home to activate your romance luck and the rituals selected for inclusion here are believed to bring fast results, especially when practiced in conjunction with other Feng Shui techniques for enhancing relationships.

three

taoist alchemy for magical relationships

element power
to enhance your personal appeal

In Feng Shui, the clever use of elemental chi – colors and combinations of colors, as well as shapes and materials – can increase or weaken energy levels to such an extent that the better or worse luck that follows becomes immediately evident. Element therapy is related to both the five elements as well as to the application of yin and yang.

To enhance the Feng Shui of your personal space you need your KUA number, which corresponds to one of the five elements. You can work out your KUA number from the formula given on page 171.

The table is the basic reference tool for personalized Feng Shui magic and shows the element, shape, and colors relating to your KUA number and the element that produces or destroys. For example, water produces wood and fire produces earth, making them supportive, while water destroys fire and metal destroys wood, which is weakening.

Elements attributes based on your KUA Number

KUA	1	2	3	4	5	6	7	8	9
Element	water	earth	wood	wood	earth	metal	metal	earth	fire
Shape	wavy	square	rectangle	rectangle	square	round	round	square	triangle
Colors	black blues	ochre yellow	green brown	green brown	ochre yellow	gold silver white	gold silver white	ochre yellow	red maroon
Productive Element	metal	fire	water	water	fire	earth	earth	fire	wood
Destructive Element	earth	wood	metal	metal	wood	fire	fire	wood	water

It is these productive and destructive elements that are the most powerfully positive or negative colors and shapes for you. So if you belong to KUA numbers 3 or 4, your element is wood, which is produced by water and hence the color that will strengthen your chi would be blues and black, and your most auspicious shape will be wavy. Based on this simple analysis, gold, metallic colors, and white would be unsuitable for wood people since, metal destroys wood. Reds and maroons are also not very good, since red exhausts wood. However, if you are wood and you were born in any of the winter months, then fire supplies the warmth you need and hence turns into a most favorable element for you.

If your number is 2, 5, or 8, your self-element is earth, and the element that produces you – and thus enhances your chi essence – is fire. At a practical level this means reds are good for you and that, generally speaking, triangular shapes strengthen you. The element that destroys earth is wood, and therefore green is not a favorable color.

When your number is 6 or 7 your self-element is metal, produced by earth, so the earth colors of yellow and ochre will make you wealthy and prosperous. Square shapes will be good for you but as fire destroys metal, it is best to avoid shades of red and triangular shapes.

Those people with number 1 have water as their self-element. Metal is the element that produces water, so white colors will favor those with water as their self-element.

If your number is 9, this indicates that your self-element is fire. The wood element produces fire, so green colors will be auspicious for fire element people.

Square shapes are lucky for those with KUA numbers 6 and 7. For numbers 2, 5, and 8, use triangular shapes to symbolically strengthen you.

round
crystal balls
for smooth relationships

Happiness in love is the result of a compatible, smooth relationship. One of the best ways of achieving this is by acquiring round crystal balls. Before use, follow a cleansing ritual and then display them in the appropriate corners of the home. They are particularly empowering in the northwest and west.

The crystal balls should be solid crystals, they can be made from natural crystal, reconstituted crystal, or even man-made lead crystals which are composed of a mixture of glass and lead. They are all effective, but not in equal measure. The best crystals are natural quartz crystals taken from deep in the earth. They should be as clear as possible.

The better-quality natural crystals usually cost twice as much as the man-made or reconstituted glass crystals, so if natural crystals are not within your budget, use clear glass spheres instead. These may not be as potent as the real thing but, nevertheless, they still signify the earth element, and the smoothness of the shapes will bring harmony to relationships between couples, and between members of the family.

Six Crystal Balls for Earth Magic

The number 6 indicates the symbol of heaven and the northwest, and it combines the intrinsic earth energy of the crystal. Six crystal balls placed in the northwest corner of the living room will bring smooth relationships between partners and favor the husband.

When the balls are placed in the southwest however, they favor the wife or matriarch. This can mean that she has the upper hand in the family and her wishes are highly respected. In the southwest corner two crystal balls will prove sufficient, because 2 is also the number of the southwest.

Placing six crystal balls in the northwest of the living room favors the man in a relationship, whereas displaying them in the southwest boosts the mother's role in the household.

Cleanse the crystal balls before you display them. To do this, soak the balls in a sea salt solution for seven days and seven nights. Afterwards, dust them each day and discourage people from touching them. You should treat your crystal balls as a store of precious energy that benefits the love relationship of the household patriarch and matriarch.

Crystals Inside the Home

Crystal balls create very useful harmonizing effects within the home. When you place a crystal ball in your lucky corners, usually the corner that is diagonal to the door or entrance into every room, and when you back this with a bright light, the room will come alive with wonderful chi.

This enhances the money making potential of residents and magnifies the amount of good luck enjoyed by everyone. Indeed the presence of crystals, especially crystal balls, always creates good energy and that is why nearly all shops selling crystals make money unless their Feng Shui is really bad.

Crystals Under the Bed

In all the bedrooms of the home, the occupants benefit from having a round crystal ball placed at the foot of the bed. This enhances the family attitudes, making everyone very happy to be part of the family. Sibling rivalry in such homes is non-existent and the relationship between the husband and wife is harmonious. In addition, the crystal under the bed also acts as a hidden talisman, with the power to contain any kind of bad luck, or negative chi that may come through the door. And, over time, as the crystal absorbs the chi of the sleeping resident, it becomes more and more powerful. If you are a spiritual person, then all the prayers you say inside your bedroom will become magnified.

Crystals under your bed have many benefits and there are practitioners who advocate using more than one crystal. Some say three crystals placed on a bed of rice attracts wealth and prosperity. Others say seven crystals, placed together with the image of a dragon tortoise, brings total protection, acting like an amulet.

Personally, I use a large bowl filled with seven crystal and semi-precious stones – citrines, amethysts, jasper, lapis lazuli, jade, turquoise, and tiger's eye. My bowl is a dragon bowl, 12 in (30mm) in diameter and my semi-precious stones are at least 1 in (25mm) across. This way I utilize all the attributes of the stones.

You can select whatever stones you wish. The important part of this ritual is that you will be using natural earth energy to

Three crystals placed on a bed of uncooked rice is a popular Chinese talisman for prosperity.

give you a good night's sleep, by making certain the surrounding energy of your bedroom is always harmonious and in a state of yin and yang balance. The crystal balls bring the harmony of a smooth flow of energy.

A Crystal Ball on the Office Desk

For those who want to accelerate their careers and use the power of Feng Shui to give them a helping hand, I urge you to invest in a round crystal ball and place this on your desk. The best place is at either end of the outside edge of the desk. If you are a woman place this crystal ball on the left side and if you are a man place it on the right hand side. Left and right are taken from your seated position.

Placing a crystal ball on your desk is an aid to excellent decision-making and concentration. Students can place a crystal globe on their desks to assist them in their studies; indeed one of my most successful tips, which has helped so many of my readers, has been to place a round crystal sphere, with the globe etched on the crystal, in the northeast corner of their children's bedrooms. This has been such an excellent energizer of study chi that many of them have written to thank me for their children becoming "A" grade students!

But remember that it is not the crystal that makes them clever, it is the crystal helping them concentrate. They are already clever! I do believe that all children are born with the potential to be "A" grade students. Just like I believe that the spark of success lies dormant in all of us until we energize it with determination and a healthy dose of yang energy. If crystals can aid in this process then crystal magic is definitely worthwhile.

Crystals as Feng Shui Cures

Crystals can be used as powerful Feng Shui cures to overcome poison arrows inside the home, also known as evil pointed peaks, that create harsh lines of killing chi. These are usually caused by the sharp corners of square pillars, furniture, tables, two walls converging, overhead beams, and the edges of overhanging beams. All these harsh lines of killing energy will make you lose money and meet with misfortune. The good news is that they are not difficult to deal with.

Feng Shui remedies usually comprise powerful objects of the five elements. Crystals belong to the element of earth, although they also contain traces of metal energy, which makes them very powerful. Thus, many types of negative energy can always be deflected using crystals.

Crystals work like mirrors, with the added advantage of having powerful earth energy of their own. So if your main front door is afflicted by a straight road pointing straight at the home, or by a triangular peak line of a neighboring roof, or by a solid wall, placing a round crystal ball on your inside wall facing outward will deflect whatever negative energy comes through the door.

Use a clear, preferably quartz, crystal ball that is at least 2-3 in (50-75mm) in diameter. Place it on a small ledge on the wall about five feet above the ground in such a position that when you open the door the first thing you see is the crystal ball. Use a smooth spherical crystal rather than a faceted crystal. And always make sure that your crystal is properly cleansed before putting it to use on the wall.

It is also a good idea to re-energize the crystal once a month. Soaking it for a few hours in sunshine water – water left in bright sunshine for at least three hours – strengthens its inner chi, making it very powerful.

I prefer to use crystals as Feng Shui cures rather than the Pa Kua mirror which is quite harmful to anyone facing it directly. Crystal balls remedy a situation without sending out bad energy because crystals possess the power to transform yin energy to yang energy by functioning as transforming agents rather than as reflective agents.

Positioning a quartz crystal ball inside your home opposite your main door will neutralize any negative chi entering the space.

amethyst magic
in the bedroom

All the different semi-precious and precious stones that represent the wealth of the earth possess a life force, which gives them important Feng Shui significance. In the same way that rock structures can be alive or dead, benevolent or malignant, so it is with semi-precious stones and crystals. And just as water is the major focus of everything to do with money and wealth luck, so too rocks, stones, and mountains – the collective components of the earth element — govern everything to do with relationships, politics, and family issues. Precious and semi-precious stones act as collectors and controllers of the life force that governs our interaction and relationships with each other.

Amethyst geodes in the bedroom generate love and help protect relationships.

The secret of powerful bedroom magic lies in the use of amethysts – the purple semi-precious stone that ranges in color from pale lilac to the deepest purple. Amethysts that are alive and possess a strong dose of yang energy are extremely powerful purveyors of earth chi. If you are lucky enough to find the right amethyst geode it can be used to keep the love and romance of your marriage well and alive forever. It could even "save" a marriage gone sour when a third party enters the relationship.

How to choose an amethyst geode

- Look for geodes with large sparkling crystals rather than small, dull-colored ones. Never use one that is chipped or cracked – this is immediately considered unlucky and should be avoided. If the amethyst breaks after it enters your home, exchange it for another.

- Choose a geode that is round or square in overall shape. These shapes suit everyone. Only fire and earth element people (check your element based on your KUA number) can benefit from the triangular-shaped geodes which signify the fire element.

- Look for a geode that is deep rather than shallow – the deeper it is, the more auspicious the geode and therefore the deeper the love in the relationship.

- Select a geode that is large enough only to balance your relationship, one that is neither too large nor too small. Larger geodes may overwhelm and small ones lack power.

- Look for a geode that appears attractive to you. It must bond with you. If you feel an instant liking for the amethyst then the stone is yours. It is obviously alive and well and will surround your space with good strong energy. If you feel indifferent, no matter how beautiful you think it is, pass on it; to bring home an amethyst geode is a serious matter, particularly if it is to be used in the bedroom.

- Amethysts are simply superb for making sure any marriage lasts. In the old days they were very popular with the wives of wealthy businessmen and merchants who often installed these stones clandestinely. These women had good reason to fear for the longevity of their marriage, since wealthy men usually took new and younger wives as they got older.

The Ritual

When you have found a suitable amethyst geode bring it home and cleanse it of all impure chi that might have been collected at the store. Place it in salt water for seven days and nights. Some masters do not like to use tap water, but I have found this to be perfectly acceptable. However, if you want the amethysts to be really cleansed, use water that has been standing in the sunlight, and thus energized by the sun, for about three hours. If there is a shower or rainstorm then it is excellent because you can then use water from heaven to cleanse your amethyst geode.

When your amethyst is ready, select an auspicious day and hour on which to move it into the bedroom by checking the Almanac. If you do not have easy access to the Chinese Almanac then do this ritual on the first or the fifteenth day of the lunar calendar. This corresponds to the days of the new moon and the full moon. Always do this ritual in the early morning hours before 11am.

Tie a red string over the base of the geode. This will symbolically awaken the amethyst as it imbues it with precious yang energy. Then take it into the master bedroom and place it under the bed.

Tie the geode with red string to the foot of the bed that is on the side that you sleep on. According to the Taoists this is a powerful protection against a husband's infidelity. If you can, try to make a male partner sleep on the left side of the bed. This means that the amethyst geode should be tied at the foot of the right side.

Make certain that the amethyst geode does not seem dead to you. A dead geode can be dangerous as it can lead to illness and lethargic energy. Amethysts should always appear brilliant and shining from within. Dead amethysts are those that appear dull, and they might have cracks and seem injured. Usually, as long as you are alert to this you will know if it is the case. Just follow your instincts.

If your amethyst looks cloudy or gathers dust, simply wiping it with a damp cloth is not enough. You have to re-energize the geode by placing it in bright sunlight, in full moonlight, or under rainwater. These are natural energizers and they bring new life to the amethyst, which in turn brings new life into your relationship.

An amethyst geode tied with red string is a powerful talisman against infidelity. It should be placed on the side of the bed occupied by the female partner, ideally on the right-hand side. The amethyst is also excellent for getting an errant husband back.

moon energy
for more marriage magic

Traditionally, good marriage luck for families meant that their sons would find suitable young women from good families who would be able to bear good strong sons to carry on the family name. For their daughters, it meant finding husbands from families that would not ill-treat her. These rituals were believed to work exceedingly fast, especially when performed correctly by young women for whom getting a kind and potentially wealthy spouse often meant a life of happy leisure.

Traditions and expectation are very different now but human nature has not changed, and there is much happiness to be gained by performing this simple means of capturing the energy of the moon. The ritual has two parts – firstly, to use moon-glow magic to enhance the sweetness of the women's looks so that anyone looking at her would find her most

Auspicious Symbols For Moon-glow Magic

The parasol protects lovers from outside interference

The double fish signifies an auspicious life together

The vase represents continuously flowing nectar to keep love alive

The lotus sustains pure love between lovers

attractive, and secondly, to use moon-glow to help her entice some young man she is already acquainted with.

To follow this ritual you will require a small and perfectly round mirror. The circular shape is exceedingly important since this is the shape of heaven. There should not be any angles to the shape of the mirror because these would symbolize and invite obstacles and problems. Roundness indicates smoothness in the potential relationship.

Ideally, the mirror should be made of gold, or at least of silver (perhaps with gold plating or gilt) and it would be even more auspicious if the mirror were to be adorned with auspicious symbols like the double happiness sign, the double fish sign, the five bats symbol, or any of the eight auspicious objects.

Other auspicious love symbols such as peonies, which are excellent, can also be molded or carved onto the mirror, which should be reasonably heavy so that it can symbolically contain the powerful accumulation of moon chi within.

The conch shell ensures fidelity despite separations

The mystic knot symbolizes never-ending love

The banner declares love to the four directions

The wheel shows that a couple may lead a blessed life together

Capturing Moon Magic

The next step in the ritual is to select an auspicious night, in accordance with the Chinese Almanac, when the moon's glow is at its zenith. The nights of the full moon are best when the sky is clear and free of clouds. On such a night bring out the mirror and shine it directly at the moon. Leave the mirror in your garden or on a high verandah or wall to absorb the light of the moon for at least three hours.

In the old days, Taoist alchemists would sit in relaxed meditation as they held a small mirror to reflect the moon-glow, knowing that such a mirror would then have been strongly energized.

Those of you who have powerful or favorite mantras can sit in meditation, quietly chanting the mantras into the mirror. The low sound of chanting will energize these small mirrors into powerful tools capable of bringing you much happiness.

When you feel that sufficient moon energy has been captured in the mirror, carefully wrap the mirror inside a silk or brocade pouch. You must never allow anyone to touch the mirror except the person who uses it. This is vital or the energy will become clouded.

You can energize a mirror and use it to help someone or you can activate a mirror to help yourself. When you have energized it, for the next fifteen nights you should use it to reflect your image so that the moon glow reflects onto your face. You will absorb the radiance and beauty of the full moon, and at the same time the mirror will become personalized with your own intrinsic energy.

When this is done you can then proceed to the second part of this ritual, which is to energize it again on the night of the next full moon. Repeat the same exercise but this time you can direct your thoughts and focus on the kind of partner you seek. Silently make a request to the God of Marriage, who is said to live on the moon, and let him send the magical moon glow of marriage into your mirror.

The mirror is now ready for use. At a propitious day and hour, find an opportunity to let the mirror reflect the face of your loved one and then let the mirror do its beautiful magic for you. The mirror does not cast a spell, it merely opens the eyes of your chosen partner to the qualities in you that were previously missed. It represents an opportunity to let the God of Marriage work some of his powerful magic.

It is not necessary to expose him or her to the mirror more than once. Also, do remember that you should only use the mirror when you are quite certain of your own feelings. Do not use the magical mirror unless you are ready for a commitment yourself.

When moon magic is used frivolously, its potency is diminished. You must also approach the whole ritual in a positive way, focusing your mind with laser-like clarity of purpose and intention. If you are lacking in concentration this ritual will be less effective. It is when your concentration is strong that moon magic lends a wonderful helping hand.

a silver box
to ask for a spouse

Another way to increase your good marriage luck is to create a special wish box and place this in the northwest or southwest corner of your bedroom. This is very auspicious if you are looking for a spouse to share your life and start a family. Select a silver box that is round or square in shape and as large or as small as you wish. Round boxes attract the luck from heaven while square shapes attract the luck of the earth. Round boxes should be kept in the northwest corner of your bedroom while square boxes should be kept in the southwest corner. These boxes can either be kept inside a cupboard or under the bed.

I once saw an antique cloisonné wish box that was as large as a chest. The lady who owned it has since passed away, but she used to tell me that the wish box brought her beloved husband to her, and indeed when I met them both they had been happily married for over thirty years. Hers had been an arranged marriage but the match had materialized soon after she had written her thoughts describing her perfect spouse and hid it inside the box. The chest was decorated with peonies, bats, and double happiness symbols. It was a beautiful cinnabar red in color, and she never tired of saying how her husband turned out to be everything she had described for herself. She has passed her special chest to her youngest daughter, who is also happily married.

I had been intrigued and charmed by the story but had forgotten it until one day my mother started telling me about the silver box ritual – how she too used to have a small silver box in which she had written her

A silver box with peony motifs, symbolizing love, can hold your wishes for the perfect soul mate.

deepest wishes. She had fallen in love with my father, she explained, and had been told about this special ritual of placing one's wish for a husband inside a silver box. So she had written my father's name inside her wish box. That was during the Japanese occupation of Malaysia when times were hard and dangerous. Nevertheless, she and my father married soon after the war was over.

It was from my mother that I have obtained this little ritual. She is a great believer in the small, square, silver box placed in the southwest.

sandalwood fan
for protection

For generations, court officials in Chinese royal households carried fans hidden in their sleeves. These fans acted as symbols of protection and many of them had powerful amulets and special mantras written on the fans that turned them into personal guardians.

Today the ritual of the sandalwood fan has long been forgotten but, as with so many traditional practices, there are old-time practitioners who continue to keep these fans and carry on the old-style magic.

Sandalwood fans are said to be especially good protectors. They enable you to deflect harmful chi, which may be sent your way by those

Fans guard against those who may be jealous of your relationship. A sandalwood-scented fan decorated with an image of a holy mountain is the traditional choice.

Fanning the body from head to toe creates the magic of protection.

jealous of your happiness with a loved one. These fans are easy to find and they are not very expensive. They often retain the distinctive fragrance of sandalwood that is said to be extremely powerful in warding off bad chi. Choose one decorated with an auspicious illustration of a holy mountain and then keep your fan as a very personal item of protection.

It is very simple to strengthen the presence of these fans in your home by using them each morning before going to work. This is a symbolic ritual that takes only a few minutes.

When you have finished your morning ablutions and just before dressing for the day, take out your sandalwood fan and, holding it high above your head, open the fan and use it to cover your body. Starting from the head, hold the fan in an open position and bring it down all the way from the top of your face down to the feet. Repeat this three times.

As you perform this ritual, symbolically think that you are using the fan to create a type of force field or shield which will surround and protect you from any harmful chi that may be directed at you.

This ritual is even more productive if you burn incense and place the fan over the incense smoke for a few moments before using it.

Chant a mantra if you know one, or chant the mantra of the compassionate Buddha: OM MANI PADME HUM. With the fan suitably energized, use it to fan your body from the head down to the toes in the way I have described, remembering to do it three times.

One thing you must do when your fan is not in use is to keep it covered and in a safe place. No one else should use it but you, so keep it hidden, out of the sight of curious children or inquisitive friends.

The fantastic power of pure yang energy simply cannot be overstated. When the essence of yang is successfully captured in a variety of ways to energize your home for different outcomes, really fascinatingly fast results will appear. The Taoists believe that boys below the age of seven embody so much pure yang energy that simply bringing them into your home and watching their behavior and reactions alone will tell you if the chi essence of your home is auspicious or not. If he falls asleep, you know that the energy can be improved. On the other hand, if he smiles and plays happily, you can be sure the chi in your home is great. And if he acts up – crying and being difficult – there is surely something amiss with the energy. Enhancing yang energy in the home can be undertaken in different ways. Try the rituals and techniques outlined here to enhance your luck.

four

powerful yang magic rituals

capture sunlight in your
magic mirror

The secret rituals of the magic mirror come from Chinese classics where references are frequently made to magical mirrors. These are imbued with special attributes which can then be used for many different purposes – for protection, for purifying intentions, and for transforming negative motivations into positive. When you capture sunlight energy in your mirror you are capturing a store of very precious and positive yang energy but, more than that, you are also accumulating powerful fire energy. It is this that enables the mirror to act as a powerful purifying agent.

Magic mirrors work best when they are circular in shape and just large enough to fit into your palm. The best mirrors are those made of gold and which have a solid feel to them, but if you do not have a gold mirror, a chrome or metallic mirror is a good substitute. It is, however, necessary to have auspicious and protective symbols behind the reflective surface. It is these symbols that help to activate the auspicious chi of the mirror. It is also important to make sure that the mirror surface itself is solid and clear and not given to misting up easily. Finally, make certain there is a handle to the mirror and that you can hold it firmly.

Consecrating the Mirror with Water or Fire Chi

When you first come across a suitable mirror that you wish to consecrate as your very own private mirror, it is a good idea to cleanse it of lingering energies picked up on its journey into your possession. This is best done using fire or water energy. To consecrate it with fire energy, use fragrant incense. Try to find good incense sticks that give off the kind of aroma you like. Use pure incense to recharge the mirror's reflective surface. This is one of the most easy and effective ways to consecrate any object, thereby making it usable in this realm of existence. Always do the incense consecration three times.

A second way of consecrating the mirror utilizes water energy. This is also a very simple procedure. Place the mirror under running tap water and then wipe it with a clean cloth. Do not use soap or a cleanser; all that is needed is yang water. Wash the mirror under the tap three times. This ritual will symbolically open the mirror's "eyes," cleanse it of any stale energy, and prepare it for use.

Choose a palm-sized, solid round mirror and cleanse it with incense or water before beginning the mirror ritual.

Activating with Sunshine Energy

On a bright sunny day you can strengthen the chi contained within the mirror using the power of sunlight. This requires a simple ritual, which involves the following steps.

Choose a good day and hour from the Chinese Almanac, making certain that your animal year (also known as the earthly branch star) does not conflict with that day. This is an important safeguard since you could fall ill if your earthly branch star is in conflict with the sunshine chi of that day.

An ancient Chinese mirror ritual involves activating sunshine energy by holding a mirror so that it catches sunlight. Always hold the mirror away from your eyes.

Using the KUA formula (see page 171) face the direction that is best for you. On a sunny day hold the mirror inside the palm of your hand and raise it high up, tilting it to catch the direct sunlight. Allow the sun to be fully reflected in the mirror.

Hold this for no longer than a maximum of nine seconds. Do not look into the mirror and always keep your eyes lowered. The sun's energy is very powerful and it can be blinding, so you must be careful not to look directly into the sun or the reflection of the sun. Also make sure you do not have people around and inadvertently tilt the mirror towards them while the sun's reflection is captured within. This could burn them. And you must not have dry paper nearby as this can catch fire. If you feel that you cannot hold the reflecting time to nine seconds, it is sufficient to hold it for six seconds. The number 9 symbolizes the power of heaven and earth. The number 6 symbolizes the power of heaven, while the numbers 2, 5, or 8 symbolize earth.

The most suitable mirrors are those available at www.wofs.com. These have been specially designed to exact specifications and can be used immediately you receive them through the mail, although you still need to activate the mirror.

Mirrors must be kept and used with respect. The usage must always be limited to that of a protective mirror or one that brings a glow of yang energy to your face. In fact, if you use your mirror to touch up your make-up or at the dressing table it is a good idea not to use it for any other purpose. Instead keep several different mirrors handy, with each one reserved for a different purpose. The mirror that is for personal use should ideally be made of gold and studded with diamonds. This brings ultimate good fortune chi.

Using the Mirror

The yang-activated mirror can be used in several different ways. Buddhists chant powerful mantras into the mirror thereby energizing it still more. If you wish to do so you can chant the Compassionate Buddha's mantra OM MANI PADME HUM 108 times each day for 108 days. This will make the mirror extremely powerful, both as a protector as well as an energizer.

The mirror is one of the most powerful antidotes against personalized poison arrows. It is thus an excellent neutralizing ritual. Below are some of the ways you can use the mirror.

If you feel that there are people within your organization who wish to undermine you, or that you are a victim of corporate politicking, you can bring the mirror to work, and slowly walk around the office reflecting the room inside the mirror, including all the people who are inside the room. Later you can take the mirror outside and by holding it up to the sunshine once, all negative intentions towards you will instantly fizzle out. The powerful yang energy will burn all bad intentions towards you and replace them with positive, loving energy.

In the course of your work, do you attend many business and corporate gatherings where there are people you meet who are your competitors, and who do not have good intentions towards you? In this case, all you need to do is give the room the "once over" with the mirror. Discreetly shine the mirror across the length and breadth and the height of the room. This will capture any negative, ill-intention towards you and neutralize it. Then, once again, take the first opportunity to place the face of the mirror to directly reflect the sun – again keeping the mirror away from your eyes – to neutralize the bad energy.

You can also use your mirror to undertake space clearing if your living or work space is being disturbed by any wandering spirit or mysterious energy mass that makes you feel uncomfortable. Reflect the mirror all around the rooms of your home. Pay particular attention to reflecting dark corners, and then immediately take the mirror outside and shine it at the sun.

Your magic mirror can also be a source of beautiful sunshine energy. Use it to reflect your face immediately after it has received the energies of the sun. Looking into the mirror and focusing briefly on your inner self will encourage your own spiritual nature to rise, filling your face with a stunning glow that makes you look and feel more beautiful. Do not use the same mirror for everything, just keep a mirror exclusively for this use.

An aggressive, competitive atmosphere at work can be dissipated by shining a mirror around the walls and corners of the company meeting room or office.

pagoda energy
for examination luck

Pagodas are said to possess the power to transform untamed and unruly minds into disciplined, well-ordered minds. As a symbol for improving the performance of the intellect it is believed to have no equal. This is probably due to the origins of the pagoda.

Many old texts describe the Chinese pagoda as having evolved from the Buddhist stupa, which symbolizes the Buddha's holy mind. Buddhists revere the stupa because this is where the cremated remains of holy lamas are kept. And even today the stupa is regarded as a holy object. They believe that circling a consecrated stupa in a

Place a pagoda in a child's room to quell boisterous behavior and promote concentration and study.

clockwise direction opens the path to enlightenment. The most famous stupa in the world has to be the Mahboudhi stupa in Bodhgaya in India, the small town where Buddha gained enlightenment under the Bodhi tree.

When Buddhism came to China the stupa slowly evolved into the pagoda and soon every little village had its own pagoda structure, usually located just outside the village. The Chinese pagoda is believed to be the place where monks are able to "imprison" cheeky spirits. There is an old legend about the white snake that transformed into a beautiful woman to ensnare an innocent young man. When a passing monk saw the woman as she really was, he set out to capture her in order to free the young man from her spell. The monk succeeded in using a pagoda to tame the snake spirit, successfully imprisoning her inside the pagoda for a thousand years.

Hence the pagoda is believed to possess the power to frighten away anything that would distract the mind. Because of this it is regarded as an excellent guardian of unruly and cheeky children – but in a beneficial way. Over the centuries, however, the pagoda has also come to be used as a symbol for enhancing the scholarly capabilities of young sons.

It is now believed that if you place a seven-tiered pagoda in the room of your child the pagoda will create the chi that leads to scholarly success, but only when it is imbued with precious yang energy. This is because pagodas are generally regarded as a yin symbol and it is only when yang chi is introduced with the presence of crimson colors that the pagoda chi is awakened. To introduce the influence of scholarly success, place a seven-tier pagoda in the northeast corner of the bedroom.

metal windchimes
cure a variety of ills

In flying star Feng Shui, a six-rod metal windchime can be used to exhaust bad chi in any afflicted sector of your home. The *wu lou* symbol means "good health."

The windchime is without doubt the most useful Feng Shui tool and I strongly recommend those keen on practicing Feng Shui have a few windchimes, especially metal ones, in the home. They are the best cures for overcoming annual star afflictions, and are also excellent for remedying a range of Feng Shui problems caused by hidden poison arrows.

All earth element afflictions, be they tangible or intangible, can be exhausted by the effect of windchime energy. This is caused by several attributes of the windchime.

The windchime that is made of metal has the power to exhaust earth, based on the cycles of the five elements. The exhausting cycle is more suitable than the destroying cycle, since complete annihilation of any element is more harmful than merely exhausting it. The idea in Feng Shui remedies is never to destroy energy of any kind, but rather to exhaust the bad energy. Since many of the more serious afflictions are the result of afflicted earth energy, metal windchimes are truly an excellent standby tool. Remember also that metal is a very yang energy and when it is big metal, this signifies the perfect yang force.

The hollow rods of the windchime create the unique situation where negative chi gets transformed into positive chi because of its movement up the hollow rod.

The sound of metal on metal is in itself a powerful antidote to negative chi. So when windchimes catch the breeze, the sound the jangling rods create is a powerful cure for any affected chi caused by intangible afflictions.

Windchimes are the most powerful cures for overcoming the illness stars of flying star Feng Shui. Under this system, the illness stars 5 and 2 are both earth element star numbers (see Chapters six and seven). Metal windchimes made from six rods and with a *wu lou* (the traditional symbol of good health) are the most powerful (see the windchime shown on the left). The number 6 symbolizes heaven and also stands for big metal. Therefore, the number 6 lends additional weight to the windchime.

The windchime can also be very useful in overcoming afflicted toilets that are located in the southwest of any home. Affliction in the southwest can be damaging to relationship luck and also hurts the matriarch of the family. Using a windchime hung inside the toilet cures the problem.

Take care not to hang windchimes directly above your head or above where you sleep, and do not hang windchimes directly above the center of doorways, as this can cause more harm than good. As a general guide the windchime should never be directly above you but should be placed at mid level along the sides of rooms and in a place where it will catch the breeze.

There is so much magic in the special singing bowls and bells that are made from seven different metals that it justifies a special chapter to delve deeper into the dimension of sounds in Feng Shui. Here we are addressing the magic of metallic sounds made beautiful through proper mixtures of metals. Nothing brings the Taoist master alchemist's science into greater focus than these special tools for space enhancement and space protection.

five

the magic of bowls and bells

singing bowl harmonics create
space magic

The use of special tools like the seven-metals singing bowl is what enables anyone to make the leap from space cleansing to space purification. The special harmonics created by the singing bowl symbolically washes all space touched by the sounds, and purifies them to a state of perfect harmony of yin and yang. This means a perfect compliment of opposite attributes: yielding with forcefulness, flexibility with firmness, and gentility with strength. When the space has been purified there is no danger of excessive yang or yin.

When yin and yang are in perfect harmony, the energy of the living space will cause occupants to behave with a firmness that is made brilliant by flexibility. There will be neither frenetic energy nor lethargy; the pace is kept even. Balance is quickly achieved, leading to higher levels of success. So when rooms and homes have been properly purified, those living in such rooms and homes enjoy greater success simply by tempering their behavior. Yin and yang often work without anyone being aware of it.

The singing bowls made by the master craftsmen of Katmandu are the best bowls to use for this purpose. These are made to conform to certain specifications which enable them to "sing" at the correct pitch and are thus excellent for transforming the chi in any space into auspicious, happy chi. The singing bowls can be used regularly to balance the energies of any home and also to awaken the human chakra points (or energy centers) within the body where soul and body connect. The singing helps to bring yang essence into the heart of any living space and, over time,

they respond to the intrinsic energies of their owners so singing bowls are always kept wrapped in soft material (preferably velvet, silk, or brocade). They should also be used regularly so that their music tunes in to the vibrations of the home.

Singing bowls are usually round metal bowls made in different sizes. To obtain the best and most gentle sounds from the bowl, it is important to place a small round cushion beneath the bowl whenever it is carried around. The cushion improves the sound of the bowl, making it purer and allowing it to ring on for longer. There is also a small wooden mallet that is actually an integral part of the ritual of the singing bowl. By tapping the bowl three times, the ringing sounds are established from which the vibrations of the room are progressively purified.

Create yin and yang harmony by purifying your space with a singing bowl.

The Quality of the Sound

This is determined by the rim thickness and resonance of the bowl; the singing vibrations depend on its depth. Singing bowls produce a wonderful pure sound when rubbed, hit, or tapped, and even a small tap with one fingernail elicits a beautiful note.

The crucible shape of bowls also serves the purpose of excellent Feng Shui; signifying a receptacle waiting to receive good sheng chi luck while simultaneously capturing and trapping all bad energy and transforming it into good energy.

To produce the special sound, the bowl should be made from seven different metals: tin, copper, zinc, iron, lead, silver, and gold, each one representing a planet and producing a different harmony. A small amount of gold incorporated into the bowls improves the sound while also symbolizing auspiciousness and giving the bowl a golden glow. Silver and gold used together represents the union of yin and yang within the bowl.

Adding Water to the Bowl

For variety of practice you might wish to put a small amount of water into the bowl and see if you like the different sound that is created when the bowl is rubbed with the mallet. To discover the particular tone that you like best, you can gradually add water, each time trying the sound. It is only by experimenting that you will be able to find the sound that has an affinity with both you and your space. If you cannot find a sound that you like by rubbing with the mallet, use the striking method.

The seven metals

Gold represents the sun, the ultimate source of yang energy

Silver represents the moon, the ultimate source of yin energy

Copper represents Venus

Iron represents Mars

Tin represents Jupiter

Lead represents Saturn

Zinc represents Mercury

Using the Singing Bowl

Before doing anything with a singing bowl, spend time getting to know it. Every singing bowl has roughly the same sound but there are slight differences in the balance of harmonics, rendering the sound of each bowl unique. Remember, too, that every space and environment is different and will make the bowl resonate differently. In addition, every person possesses his or her own energies, which also change from moment to moment. The same bowl could well sound different at different times.

Also, note that as your living space becomes purified with regular use, the singing sounds emitted each day will become purer, clearer, and sharper, reflecting the cleaner energies of the air around you. Develop an awareness of these improvements.

Place the singing bowl on its cushion on your upturned left palm. Spend a few seconds tuning in to the heaviness of the bowl.

The gold in a singing bowl represents the sun.

Take up the wooden mallet and gently strike the rim of the bowl with it. Each person will hear a different kind of humming, singing sound. Some will hear deep undertones followed by a throbbing sound while others will focus on undulating overtones. Close your eyes, allowing yourself to enter the sound waves created. Experiment with the way you strike the bowl and you will discover many delightful surprises.

Over time, you will become familiar with the bowl and feel the vibrations. Eventually, through the tones and undulating vibrations, you will be able to detect the initial disharmonies that after a small period of time become more harmonious. The sound itself will balance the chi in the surrounding space, and once the energies become balanced, the bowl sings melodiously. It converts the wonderful auspicious chi around the space into a delightful humming sound that soothes and calms.

The silver in a singing bowl symbolizes the moon.

The Singing Bowl Purification Ritual

Singing bowl therapy can be done as often as you like. When you undertake this practice, focus your mind and concentrate clearly on what you are doing. I usually use singing bowl therapy only after purifying my space with incense. This aligns the energies within the living space and appeases any spirits that may be there. The home will then be filled with yang energy that is pure and balanced, especially when special mountain incense is used. It is then that immense harmony is created. On the days when you do these space purification rituals, everyone will move around the home with a smile.

This ritual is simple but effective in creating a very calming influence. If you are new to this practice, my advice is to do it once every ten days.

Start by placing the bowl on a small cushion and, resting it on your left palm, walk slowly from room to room. Strike the bowl three times with the mallet each time you enter a room and move in a clockwise direction around each of the rooms. For the purposes of space purification, you need to aim for a continuous, clear or humming sound as you move with the bowl from room to room and from door to door. Striking the rim of the bowl three times creates the first set of sounds. Let the sound ring out loud and follow its resonance. As the sound begins to fade, strike again, and keep doing this as you move around the room. Stay close to the walls of each room so that any unbalanced energy that is stuck to the walls will be distilled and refined by the sheer purity of the sound. When you come to doors and windows, circle the bowl three times to reinforce the purification process.

Another way to make the bowl ring is to rub the mallet around the rim of the bowl in a clockwise direction. Keep a firm tension on the mallet and listen as a gentle humming sound grows in intensity. If you cannot get the bowl to sing, first try striking the bowl to wake it up and then start rubbing the rim. The trick is in the tension with which you hold the mallet and press against the rim. Press the rim evenly and firmly. Once you are good at making your bowl sing, the sheer beauty of the sound will carry you away.

If you have a room that you consider to be especially unlucky, place the bowl on a table with the cushion underneath. Let the bowl steady itself and then strike the rim of the bowl with the wooden mallet, letting the pure sound travel around the room.

For enhanced purification, simultaneously chant mantras that you are familiar with – the best one for this purpose is the lovely and wonderful mantra of compassion OM MANI PADME HUM.

Take your singing bowl and mallet and work through each room of the home in a clockwise direction, striking the bowl three times at intervals.

The sound of temple bells emits harmonious, uplifting energy.

The Importance of Sound Rituals in Feng Shui

It is believed that all things – including buildings, mountains, and hills – emit energy and have their own sounds, but that this changes, depending on the quality of chi around it at any given moment.

The scientific explanation is that all things are a collection of atoms that dance and produce sounds by their movements. When the atoms are in harmony, the sounds produced are pure and melodious. It is said that in the beginning, the wind created everything on earth and atoms danced ceaselessly, producing songs that were both creative and auspicious as well as sounds that were destructive, causing disintegration.

The use of sounding objects is an ancient practice in Eastern countries because sound can be used to soothe the energies of any living space, encouraging balance and harmony. Temple bells, drums, gongs, and other instruments were also often used in space blessings and other rituals.

In Feng Shui ritual, singing bowl purification has many benefits:

- enhancing the energies of the living space
- transforming inauspicious energies into auspicious energies
- activating the element energies of particular corners.

In addition, many people feel uplifted after a space has been bathed with the harmonics of a singing bowl. The humming tone of the bowl instills feelings of profound peace, the explanation being that the ultrasonic sound waves internally massage the human psyche, evoking a feeling of relaxed well-being. Externally, it soothes the vibrations and wavelengths of the living space, creating the harmony that attracts good fortune.

magic bells
attract yang energy

Specially made singing bells work in a similar way to singing bowls. Their sounds purify the space, bathing it with balanced yin and yang energy. Both singing bowls and bells have the ability to attract yang energy from the ten directions towards them.

Like singing bowls these small golden bells are also made from seven types of metal representing the 7 planets. They signify the element of metal from heaven and they improve and become more potent with regular use. The more you use these bells to start all your Feng Shui rituals the more yang energy they are able to attract; needing only to be rung lightly to release the harmonics of tinkling, lingering sound which instantly attracts people to it. The purity of the sound depends on the space itself and on the person ringing the bell.

Ringing bells attract yang energy for Feng Shui rituals.

There are also special mantras which can be chanted over the bells to enhance their power to attract. My most holy lama has given me permission to share this perfect mantra, which is meant specially for waking up the spirit of your bells. If you should get a special bell you can consecrate it by chanting this mantra, seven times over the bell: OM PADMO USHNISHA VIMALE HUM PHAT.

Chanting this mantra over the bells also means that each time the bell is rung, blessings emanate from the bell into the ten directions.

You can bring amazing potency to your Feng Shui practice by harnessing the magic of "flying" numbers. The numbers 1 to 9 are known by Chinese masters as flying stars, and these help explain the effect of time-dimension Feng Shui – or how the luck of your home changes year by year, according to the Chinese Hsia calendar. Flying Star Feng Shui is one of the most powerful Feng Shui techniques of the compass school you can employ. The numbers 1 to 9 have different meanings and represent the code of the ancients. They signify the quality of good luck in certain corners as well as different kinds of bad luck. The key to Flying Star Feng Shui is knowing how to interpret these numbers. Flying numbers are expressed in specially-formulated natal charts, which offer suggestions on how to manage the magical energies of your living spaces.

six

the magic
of flying
numbers

lucky
and unlucky flying numbers

There is wonderful potential for creating the magic embodied in the flying numbers of one of the most powerful systems of feng shui. Chinese Feng Shui masters refer to the numbers 1 to 9 as flying stars. These stars move around the sectors in a pre-determined order according to the time cycle of the lunar calendar. Each number possesses intrinsically auspicious or inauspicious meanings – lucky or unlucky – although the luck of these numbers can also transform from good to bad and bad to good,

The number 1 is extremely lucky, particularly when located in the north and activated by a water feature such as an aquarium.

Number 6 represents heaven, symbolized by the trigram Chien shown here. The luck of 6 is magnified by metal. Creating a silver wish box (see Tip 19) is best done under the influence of 6.

Brilliant relationship luck, represented by the double happiness symbol, is the bounty of number 8, plus the arrival of great money luck. To benefit from number 8, boost the elements of water and earth.

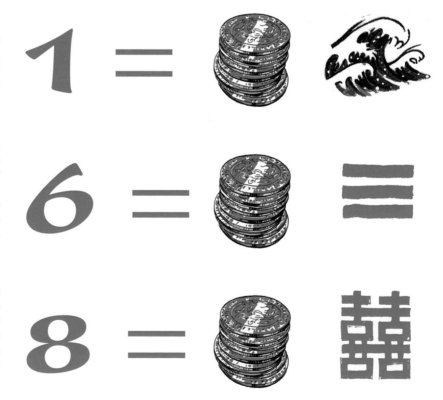

depending on which sector of the house they occupy. Familiarity with these flying numbers and the specially formulated natal charts will bring enormous benefit to your practice of feng shui. As you learn to understand the natal chart of a home, you will discover how to manipulate the intangible energies that flow through living spaces from day to day.

The Lucky Numbers

The three luckiest numbers are 8, 6, and 1. These are known as the white star numbers. When they occur singly or together in the same compass sector, they indicate good fortune in that part of the house or room.

Of all the lucky numbers, the luckiest number is 8. It indicates good fortune that is about to arrive. Indeed, on February 4, 2004, we will enter the period when 8 becomes the ruling number and, for the next 20 years, the number 8 will be exceedingly lucky. We can perform powerful magic with this number in two areas of our life – relationship luck and wealth luck. We can also use it to prevent the onset of illness.

We do this by using the natal charts of houses to locate where the flying water star 8 and the flying mountain star 8 are placed. Different homes have their auspicious water and mountains stars located in different sectors, depending on the orientation of their home. When you know where these two very significant flying numbers are located, it is possible to enhance relationship and wealth luck by strengthening the mountain and water stars. By activating the number 8 water star effectively you will create fantastic money luck in your living space, and by strengthening the number 8 mountain star you will find that your social life becomes more active and your love life is vastly improved. This is what you will learn to do in this chapter.

Number 1 is an incredibly lucky number, especially when it flies into the north as the water star. If your home enjoys this situation and the front door is located here, or if the bedroom you occupy is located in this sector, you will enjoy excellent career luck. Whichever corner it occupies, the number I water star can still bring plenty of success luck if it is energized by the strategic placement of a water feature, which strengthens its element nature.

Heaven and the family breadwinner are both number 6. When it is located and then activated with either a metallic windchime or something made of precious metal like gold or silver, the fortunes of the family will be significantly enhanced. This is also when it will be most beneficial to create your silver box of secret wishes (see Tip 19).

The numbers 1,6, and 8 are all potent wealth bringers. Number 7 is also lucky, but only until the end of period 7 in 2004. In coin rituals, multiples of 3 are fortuitous.

The number 4 brings success in the literary and creative fields, and under most circumstances, also brings amazing romance luck with many social and love opportunities arising, and even marriage possibilities. However, when there is excessive water nearby, the 4 misbehaves and this can lead to scandals associated with illicit sexual affairs!

The number 7 is currently a lucky number, although it is lucky only until the changeover to the period of 8, which happens on February 4, 2004. After that date the number 7 ceases to be auspicious and becomes a dangerous star number, representing violence.

The Unlucky Numbers

Numbers that are unlucky are not merely inauspicious. These are numbers that often represent misfortunes of the most severe kind, so they can be dangerous. They should always be taken seriously.

The most dangerous number is 5, which usually signifies accidents, illness, and financial loss. The number 2 can also bring illness. Number 3 is the quarrelsome number, bringing lawsuits and misunderstandings that can have unfortunate consequences. When these numbers occur singly their potency is considerably reduced, but the bad luck increases when they occur together and, if any of them meet up and combine with the number 9, the bad luck and misfortunes are multiplied many times over.

The number 7 is usually inauspicious and very unlucky, but when it is the reigning number it transforms into an auspicious number. Since we are currently in the period of 7 it is considered lucky, but as we change to the period of 8 in 2004, the number 7 will revert to an unlucky star that attracts violence, bloodshed, and robbery.

Windchimes are effective cures for misfortune caused by unlucky numbers.

the feng shui
natal chart

Enhancing the glitter of auspicious flying numbers and exhausting, or dousing, the dangerous numbers constitutes a powerful and magical dimension to the practice of Feng Shui. But this usually requires intimate knowledge of the school of Feng Shui known as Three period (or Sarn yuan) Feng Shui, and learning how to cast the natal charts of homes and buildings. The process of teaching a student how to do this has always been both arduous and long, but today this learning has been cleverly condensed and the process enormously simplified. Passing on the secrets of old knowledge that were once the exclusive domain of the old masters has become much easier.

Feng Shui masters construct natal charts of buildings by plotting the way the numbers 1 to 9 fly from one compass sector of the house to another. The flight path of the star numbers are based on what is called the Lo Su Square of nine numbers.

In the original Lo Shu Square (left) you will see that the number 5 is in the center. The ascending number from 5, which is 6, is placed in the grid marked by the direction northwest. The number 7 is in the

The flight path of star numbers on the Lo Shu Square.

SE   S   SW

E   W

NE   N   NW

grid marked west, and the number 8 is in the grid marked northeast. If you follow the ascending numbers you will begin to see that there is a rather complicated flight path. The numbers actually jump from sector to sector. Everyone practicing Sarn yuan Feng Shui method has this flight path committed to memory.

The numbers in the original Lo Shu Square are very special. The ancient texts refer to it as the magic square of Chinese Feng Shui. Adding together any three numbers of the grid in any direction makes the sum of 15, and it takes 15 days for the moon to go through one waxing or waning cycle and progress from new moon to full moon. The number 15 is significant to the lunar calendar, and it is this that makes this grid so important in the context of time dimension feng shui. Hence Taoist scholars and master alchemists regard the Lo Shu Square as the key to unlocking feng shui's many exciting secrets, formulas, and rituals.

Casting a Natal Chart

The masters take account of the year when a building or house was constructed or last renovated; this implies major work that involved additional floor space or other structural work, and not merely repainting or redecorating. Therefore, it is vital that you find out the provenance of your home.

Secondly, Feng Shui masters take very accurate measurements of the direction that the house or building faces. The facing direction usually means the direction the main door faces, although sometimes it can also refer to the direction of maximum yang energy (such as a main road) or to the orientation of the house or building, which may not be the same as the main door direction.

determining
orientations

The Three Ways to Determine Orientations

Generally, we consider the orientation of any building by determining what direction the building is facing. We can also consider the source or direction of the most "yang" energy. This is usually the main road.

Thirdly, and most importantly, we consider where the main door is facing and use this as the orientation unless the main door is facing a garage, or a wall away from the main road. To avoid confusion, we define the main door as being the door most frequently used by the residents.

Taking a Compass Reading

All you will need to do is take accurate measurement of your front door direction, then carefully read the degrees off the compass to determine the category of your house.

It is very worthwhile to invest in a good, reliable compass. The more detailed the readings, the better it will be. Always take readings at the main door, standing inside and facing out. Take the reading three times for accuracy, and do this from positions about a foot apart, maybe higher and lower and inside the house. If any electrical products are disturbing the compass, remove them first before taking the reading again. From the reading of the orientation you will be able to determine the house category.

What Category House?

Once you know your house category, you will be able to identify the natal chart that applies to your house or building. You will notice on the chart on page 120 that the flying star system splits each of the eight directions into three sub directions, making a total of 24 directions. Thus we have South 1, 2, and 3 and so on. The natal charts for the second and third sub directions are similar, so there is a total of 16 natal charts, which will cover all the houses in any one period.

The Natal Charts

In the following section I have precalculated the natal charts for all 16 categories of houses that were built or renovated between February 4, 1984 and 2004. These are described as Period 7 houses.

The charts are illustrated by house plans, showing how to activate the lucky wealth and relationship sectors of each. By the time you have studied all sixteen of the illustrations, you will have developed an easy familiarity with the use of numbers and know how to superimpose the placement of these numbers onto homes to find out how to improve your wealth and relationship luck sectors.

In a, the orientation of the house is determined by the direction of the main door. In b, the main door faces a garage, so instead the house is orientated as shown by the arrow. In c, the house appears to be facing the same way as the other two, but its main door is on the side of the house, so in this case the orientation matches that of the main door.

Find your house category

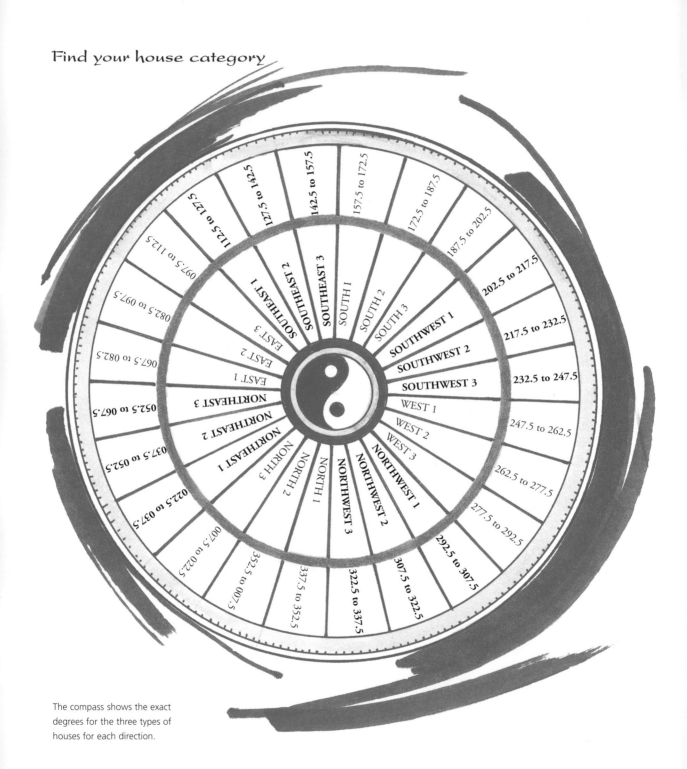

The compass shows the exact degrees for the three types of houses for each direction.

The facing direction of the main door of the whole apartment block, rather than that of your own apartment door, determines the building's natal chart.

Special words for apartment dwellers

- If you live in an apartment you should take the direction of the main door to the building to identify the natal chart of the whole building. Do not forget to check when the building was built, or when it was last renovated.

- You then identify where your apartment is located in the sense of in which compass sector of the building your apartment is located. This will immediately give you the general luck of your apartment.

- In this school of feng shui there is also the concept of big chi and small chi. The big chi refers to the whole Lo Shu Square superimposed on the whole building. The small chi refers to the same Lo Shu Square superimposed on individual apartments and individual rooms.

- To investigate the particular luck of your apartment, you must identify its direction and, using the same natal chart, superimpose it onto your apartment so that you will be able to identify the different sectors inside your apartment for the purpose of analyzing your Feng Shui.

- This is also the method to use when you read all the remedies being given to take care of afflicted corners. You can also use this technique to identify which sectors have been visited by auspicious flying star numbers and therefore need to be activated.

analyzing element
relationships

In addition to the intrinsically lucky and unlucky meanings, each of the numbers also has a matching element. The number 1 is water; 2, 5, and 8 are earth; 3 and 4 are wood; 6 and 7 are metal; and 9 is fire. The element attribute of each of the numbers offers additional insights into the way numbers affect the living space. The element dimension also enables the practitioner to correct bad luck corners, and to enhance the good luck corners.

The following illustrations of homes and natal charts highlight two important types of luck – income and relationship luck – which anyone can implement. These are indicated by the auspicious water star numbers, which bring wealth, and auspicious mountain star numbers, which bring beneficial relationships. The water star is the number at the top right of the main number in each square, and the mountain star is on the top left.

Both of these star numbers can be activated as soon as you know where lucky stars are situated in your home. The locations are always expressed in terms of compass sectors. The auspicious water and mountain stars are the star numbers 8. From the examples, you can therefore see how you can then apply the natal chart information to your own home.

The three element cycles: the Destructive Cycle (the inner star), the Exhaustive Cycle (the outer ring), and the Productive Cycle (inner ring).

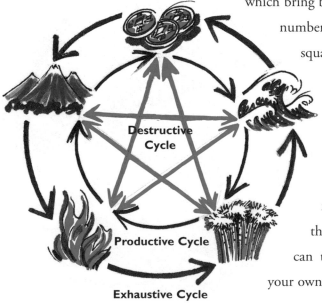

Destructive Cycle

Productive Cycle

Exhaustive Cycle

When you look at the different natal charts, you can also examine the interaction of the elements, which are symbolized by the different numbers and the compass sectors. The influences of the elements are summarized here as guidelines to show how you can interpret the numbers that appear in each of the eight sectors. This enables you to understand the meanings of the numbers according to the productive and destructive cycles of the elements.

water

In the north sector (water): 1 is very good, and when 6 or 7 comes into the north it is even better, because metal produces water. 3 or 4 tires out the chi of the sector so it is exhausting, but 2 or 5 destroys the chi here, which is not good. But when 8 comes in, the luck of this number overrides the element relationship.

wood

In the east and southeast sectors (wood): when 3 or 4 comes into either sector, it is good. When 1 comes in it is even better, as water produces wood. If 6 or 7 comes in it is fatal, and when 9 flies in, it exhausts the chi of these sectors.

In the south sector (fire): when 9 comes into the sector it is good. When 3 or 4 comes in, it is even better. When 1 comes in it is destructive, and when 2 or 5 flies in, the chi gets exhausted.

fire

In the southwest and northeast sectors (earth): 2, 5, or 8 is good, and when 9 flies in it is even better, because fire produces earth. The bad numbers for this sector are 1, which is destructive, and 6 and 7, which exhaust the sector.

earth

In the west and northwest (metal): 6 or 7 brings harmonious luck. When 2, 5, or 8 comes in it is great because earth produces metal but the fire number 9 can have disastrous effects, and when 1 flies in, the chi here gets exhausted.

metal

natal charts
of the current period

The following natal charts show the effect of the flying star numbers for homes with their main doors facing the 16 cardinal and secondary directions and their sub directions. I have included as many different types of home as possible in order to show the varying ways in which the natal charts can be applied.

Note that for some multi-level homes, the natal chart changes for each floor. This is because often the ground floor may occupy a larger space due to a garage or extension, so the grid sectors take up a smaller space on upper floors. Also, the house facing direction literally means that of the whole house; don't be confused by the location of the main door on some of the following plans. Just because a main door faces a particular direction, it does not always mean that the main door always falls in the same grid sector. For example, a north-facing house can have a main door that is located in the northeast sector. To remind you of this, a small house symbol is included on each natal chart, and floor plans are labeled where it occurs.

Throughout, two key symbols are used on the floor plans:

The crystal symbol represents the earth element, and shows where you can harness the energy of the lucky mountain star (1, 6, 7, and 8), using energizers such as crystals, crystal geodes, and boulders.

 The fish symbol denotes where you can activate the auspicious water star, using yang water features such as aquariums, fountains, ponds, and waterfalls.

A north 1-facing house (337.5 to 352.5°)

SE	S	SW
3 2 **6**	7 7 **2**	5 9 **4**
4 1 **5**	2- 3+ **7**	9 5 **9**
8 6 **1**	6 8 **3**	1 4 **8**
NE	N	NW

E (left), W (right)

1 Your most lucky sector is the northeast where all three numbers 1, 6, and 8 are lucky. And if your door is located here but facing north, you will enjoy great popularity and smooth relationships, because the mountain star 8 is located in this corner. Wealth luck is also very inspiring because the water star is 6, also a lucky number. As 6 is metal and metal produces water, this is doubly auspicious.

2 Activate the mountain star in the northeast by having a chunky crystal here, a boulder, or a globe image.

3 The water star 8 is located in the north so a water feature here will bring awesome wealth luck. If there is a door located here, place the water to the left of the door (inside looking out).

4 The northwest sector is auspicious, and this part of the house is suitable for students. Place a metal painting here to energize luck from heaven.

5 The south sector has the auspicious double 7, so anyone occupying the south bedroom will enjoy good luck. However, the southeast sector has the quarrelsome stars 3 and 2, so anyone in the southeast bedroom will suffer relationship conflicts. Use a blue color scheme to overcome this affliction.

bedroom · bedroom · living area · kitchen · dining area

**Main door faces north
1 in the northeast
sector**

A north 2/3-facing house (352.5 to 022.5°)

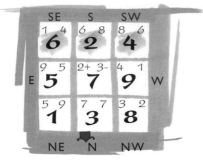

1 Here, the southwest enjoys the auspicious stars 8, 6, and 4. This includes the mountain star 8, so placing a large crystal or earth object here will be most auspicious. Unfortunately, the southwest is occupied by the toilet, so this very lucky sector is wasted.

2 The south has the auspicious water star 8. But here the south is occupied by the kitchen and bathroom, so this is a real waste. If your bedroom is here place a water feature just outside the bedroom door.

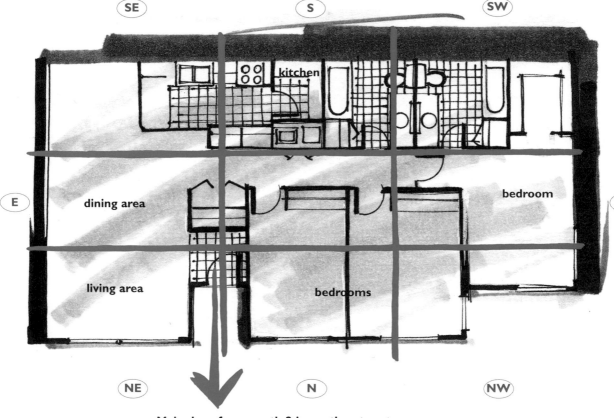

Main door faces north 2 in northeast sector

3 The southeast has the excellent 4/1 combination, and this brings good luck for those in the communications industry, and for writers and scholars.

4 Both the dining and living areas of this house are badly afflicted by the inauspicious combination of the 5/9, so hanging windchimes in these rooms will make a huge difference to the luck of the house.

A south 1-facing house   (157.5 to 172.5°)

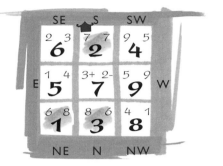

1 Your water star 8, which brings enhanced income luck and more money, is located in the northeast sector. Placing a water feature here brings prosperity and many new sources of income. But if your bedroom is located here, as shown in this example, then you should not place water in the bedroom. If there are two levels to your home and there is a living room on one level of this sector, energize with a flowing water feature.

2 The mountain star 8 is located in the north. If you place a beautiful crystal here it will greatly enhance your love life. But if you have a toilet placed in this sector, as shown in this example, all the good love luck simply gets washed away.

3 The southeast has the quarrelsome and ill-health stars, so it is a good idea to leave this part of the building alone. If your bedroom is here in the southeast, do not use a windchime – just make this area very quiet.

Main door faces south 1

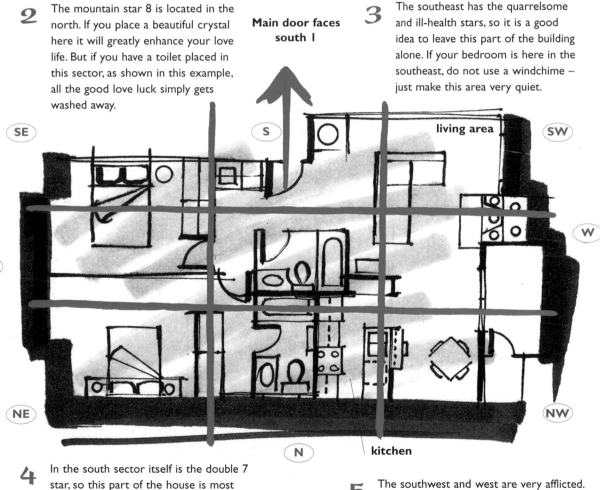

4 In the south sector itself is the double 7 star, so this part of the house is most lucky, but only until February 4, 2004.

5 The southwest and west are very afflicted. Place six-rod windchimes in rooms here.

A south 2/3-facing house (172.5 to 202.5°)

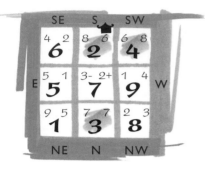

	SE	S	SW
	4 2 **6**	8 6 **2**	6 8 **4**
E	5 1 **5**	3- 2+ **7**	1 4 **9**	W
	9 5 **1**	7 7 **3**	2 3 **8**
	NE	N	NW

1 The water star 8 is located in the southwest sector of this house. On the ground floor it is wasted, as the southwest houses the garage and upstairs, on the first floor, it is partly missing. I suggest a waterfall in the southwest garden, and that the bedroom 3 window upstairs is opened to capture some of the auspicious chi.

Main door faces south 2/3

SE S SW

E W

NW

NE N

garage

living area

dining area   kitchen   living room

2 The mountain star 8 is in the south, where the main front door is making the house very auspicious. This is because the water star here is 6, which is also a lucky number. Place a beautiful amethyst here to create amazing popularity luck for residents. Upstairs, the master bedroom benefits from the good star numbers because it is partly in the south sector.

3 The north sectors are also auspicious because of the double 7. On the ground floor, the kitchen placed here does not take advantage of the lucky double 7, but upstairs the persons occupying bedroom 2 will enjoy good fortune until February 4, 2004. It is not even necessary to activate the chi here, because the room sits squarely in the north grid of the chart.

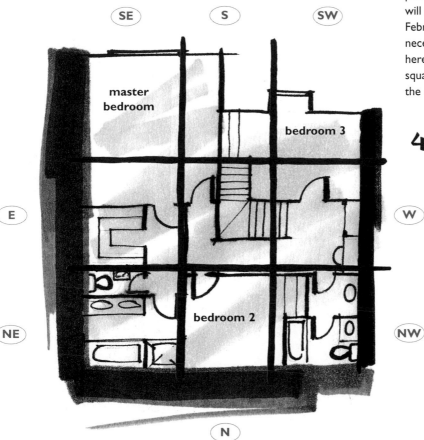

4 The east and northeast are said to be seriously afflicted sectors. The east has the five yellow as the mountain star, and the main period number is also 5. On the ground level this afflicts the living room, so it is necessary to hand a six-rod windchime there to overcome the effect of the double 5. Upstairs, the master bedroom is affected so a large metallic windchime must be hung by the bedroom door.

5 The northeast has the 9/5 combination which also needs to be remedied with something metallic. Downstairs, the dining room falls in this northeast sector, so it is a good idea to hang a metal painting here or place six coins on the wall or under the carpet. Upstairs, the bathroom falls in this sector, which neutralizes the bad numbers.

6 The northwest is afflicted by horrible fighting star numbers. The 2/3 combination leads to loud quarrels between residents. This place must be kept very quiet, and use the "red and gold" cure – hang a red and gold painting there to calm the fighting stars. Downstairs, the living room in in this sector, so it is vital to have red and gold here too. Upstairs in the bathroom, the 2/3 stars are harmless.

An east 1-facing house (067.5 to 082.5°)

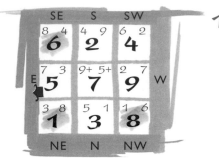

	SE	S	SW	
	8 4 **6**	4 9 **2**	6 2 **4**	
E	7 3 **5**	9+ 5+ **7**	2 7 **9**	W
	3 8 **1**	5 1 **3**	1 6 **8**	
	NE	N	NW	

1 Hang a six-rod windchime in the center of the home. If you have toilets and bathrooms here they will press down on the bad luck of this part of the house where the flying numbers are inauspicious.

2 The auspicious water star 8 is in the northeast sector. If this sector is not occupied by your bedroom and is inside the home, you can activate it with an aquarium. In this example, half the auspicious sector is missing as it lies outside the house.

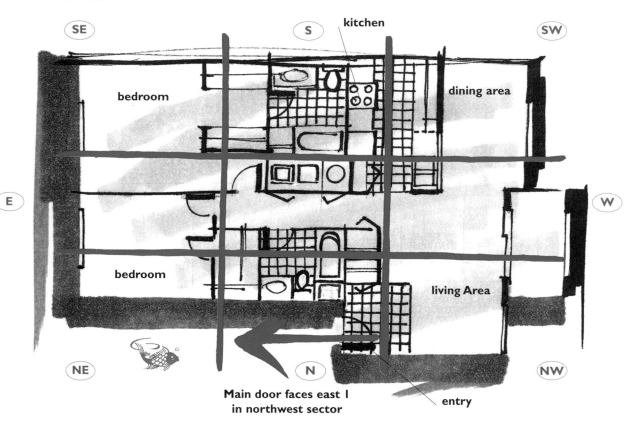

Main door faces east 1 in northwest sector

3 The mountain star 8 is in the bedroom located in the southeast sector. This sector is also auspicious because the other numbers here (main number 6 and secondary water number 4) are also auspicious.

4 The main door is located in the northwest sector, which has the lucky combination of 1, 6, and 8 bringing luck to this house. If your northwest corner houses your bedroom or living room it is most auspicious. If it houses your toilet or kitchen, then your luck has been pressed down.

An east 2/3-facing house (082.5 to 112.5°)

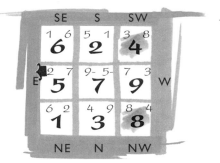

1 The water star 8 has flown to the southwest sector of the home. In this example the southwest corner is missing. If the outside is the garden, the auspicious water star can be activated by installing a water pond and opening a window facing the pond from the dining room. Wealth will then increase by leaps and bounds.

2 The bedroom in the north sector is affected by the 4/9 combination. The strengthened fire element in the north creates restless energy. Paint the bedroom blue.

3 The mountain star 8 is in the northwest sector in this example, partly outside the home. Place a big boulder here to create relationship magic. Tie the boulder with a red string or ribbon. If your mountain star 8 is inside your home you can display a large crystal in this corner to benefit from the luck of the earth.

4 The door is situated in a very unlucky sector (the east itself). A windchime hung here will dissipate all the bad luck of the flying numbers. The center of the home also needs a metal windchime.

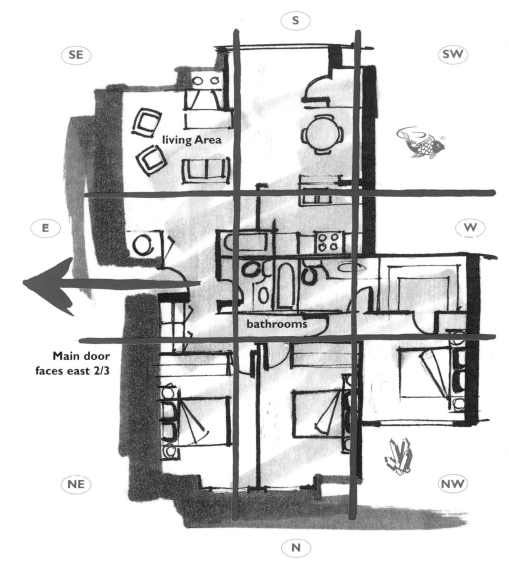

A west 1-facing house (247.5 to 262.5°)

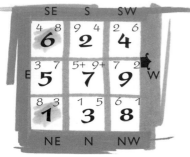

1 Auspicious water star 8 is in the southeast corner of the house, occupied by the living area. Placing a water feature here, both inside and outside the house, would be auspicious for prosperity luck. Make sure the window stays open to receive the wealth chi that is activated.

2 The auspicious mountain star 8 falls in the northeast of the home where the bedroom is located. Placing a crystal in this part of the home will activate this auspicious star.

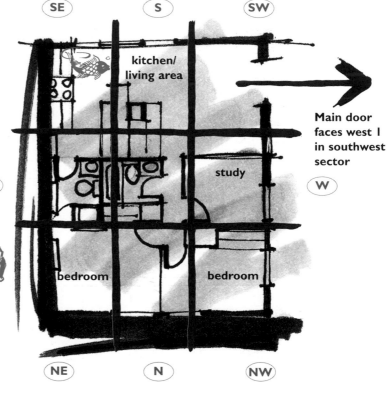

You can energize the auspicious 8 water star using water features such as a fish pond, aquarium, or fountain. If possible, seek out the awesome Feng Shui fish, the arrowana, for its beautiful, wealth-attracting gold scales. The auspicious 8 mountain star can be energized with crystals, stones, and boulders, or a picture of a mountain, which symbolizes earth luck.

3 The main door faces west but it is located in the southwest, where it benefits from the water star 6.

A west 2/3-facing house   (262.5 to 292.5°)

1 The auspicious water star of this house is located in the northwest corner, which is an ideal place to have a waterfall. Build an artificial waterfall in this part of the garden and let the water fall towards the house entrance. Wealth luck is activated. There are special ways to design a waterfall that is auspicious (see Tip 8), and if you wish you can also place a wealth god in the waterfall to create prosperity magic. The most vital thing is to make sure the water is flowing towards the house and not away from it, and that the water is clean.

2 The auspicious mountain star 8 is located in the southwest and this is an excellent feature since energizing the southwest for relationship luck now becomes doubly potent. So place a singularly large crystal in this corner or, if you like, a decorative boulder will do just as well. This will enhance all the relationships in your life.

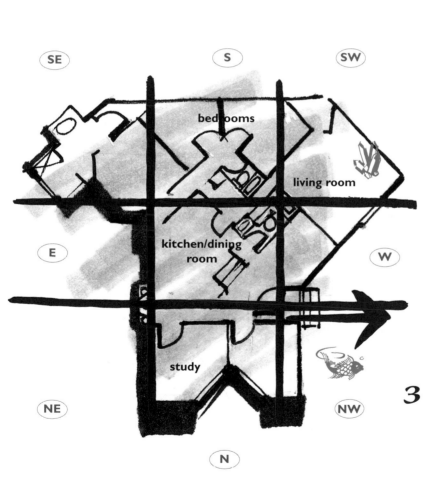

Main door faces west 2/3 in northwest sector

3 The unlucky sectors are the south and the east. In the south, place windchimes to overcome the accident stars; and in the east there is no need to worry because this sector is missing in this irregularly-shaped house.

A northeast 1-facing house (022.5 to 037.5°) **GROUND FLOOR**

SE	S	SW
5 9 **6**	9 5 **2**	7 7 **4**
6 8 **5**	4- 1+ **7**	2 3 **9**
1 4 **1**	8 6 **3**	3 2 **8**
NE	N	NW

E (left side)   W (right side)

1 In this house, note that on the ground level the east is occupied by a living room so placing a water feature here (like an aquarium) would attract wealth luck into the house. In the upper level there is bedroom 3. Here there is no need to put a water feature – in fact it is not advisable to do so. Just staying here in this room will bring good luck.

Note how the Lo Shu grid has been superimposed onto the house to make analysis easier. Study the numbers and match them correctly to the respective grid areas.

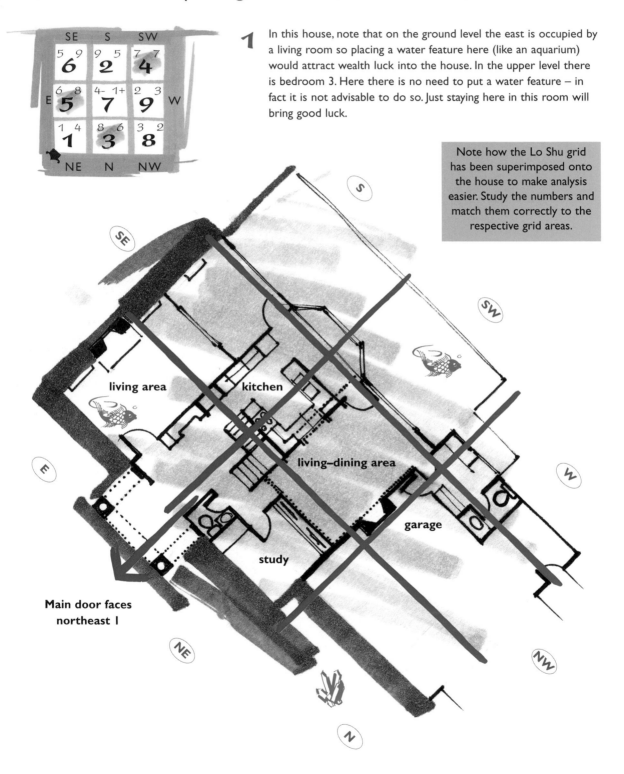

living area

kitchen

living–dining area

garage

study

Main door faces northeast 1

2 The auspicious mountain star 8 is located in the north sector. So if a stone garden filled with decorative boulders is built outside the study it would create good fortune for the residents, or there can be a decorative wall built here. Upstairs the main bedroom is placed here in the north. This is excellent and simply placing a crystal here would make the couple's marriage happier and more auspicious.

3 Note that the southeast and south are plagued by the afflicted 5/9 combination. The south sector is especially dangerous so, ideally, the bedroom should not be used. It can stay as a guest bedroom, as anyone living here would get ill; the cure is a windchime.

4 Another excellent feature of this house is that the quarrelsome star combinations of 2/3 and 3/2 in the west and northwest are in the garage. This means they will not play havoc with the family living here as these bad stars are regarded as being outside the home.

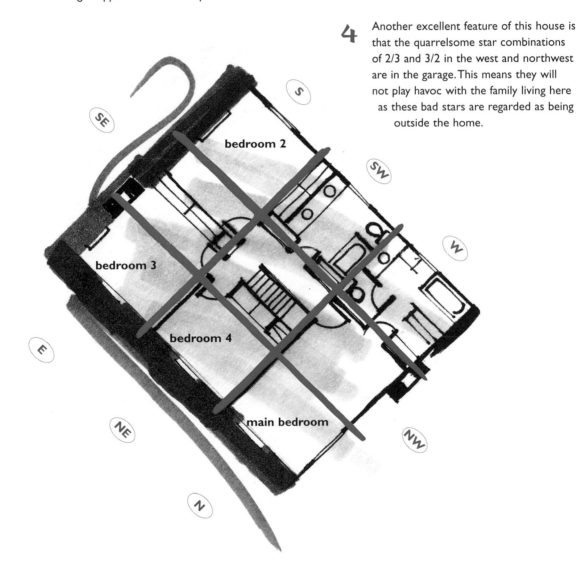

A northeast 2/3-facing house (037.5 to 067.5°)

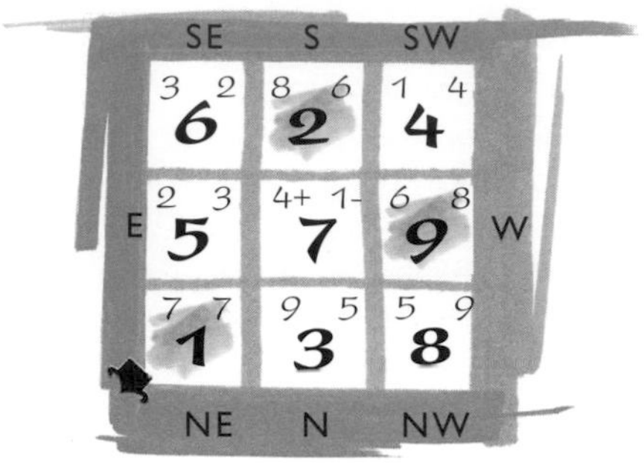

1 The auspicious water star 8 is located in the west corner of this home. If you energize this part of the home with a water feature like a small fountain or an aquarium, it will activate money luck for the residents.

2 The auspicious mountain star 8 is located in the south sector. Inside the home the energy of this part of the house can be stimulated with a dark-colored earth material. Semi-precious stones, like tiger's eye, will be most auspicious here.

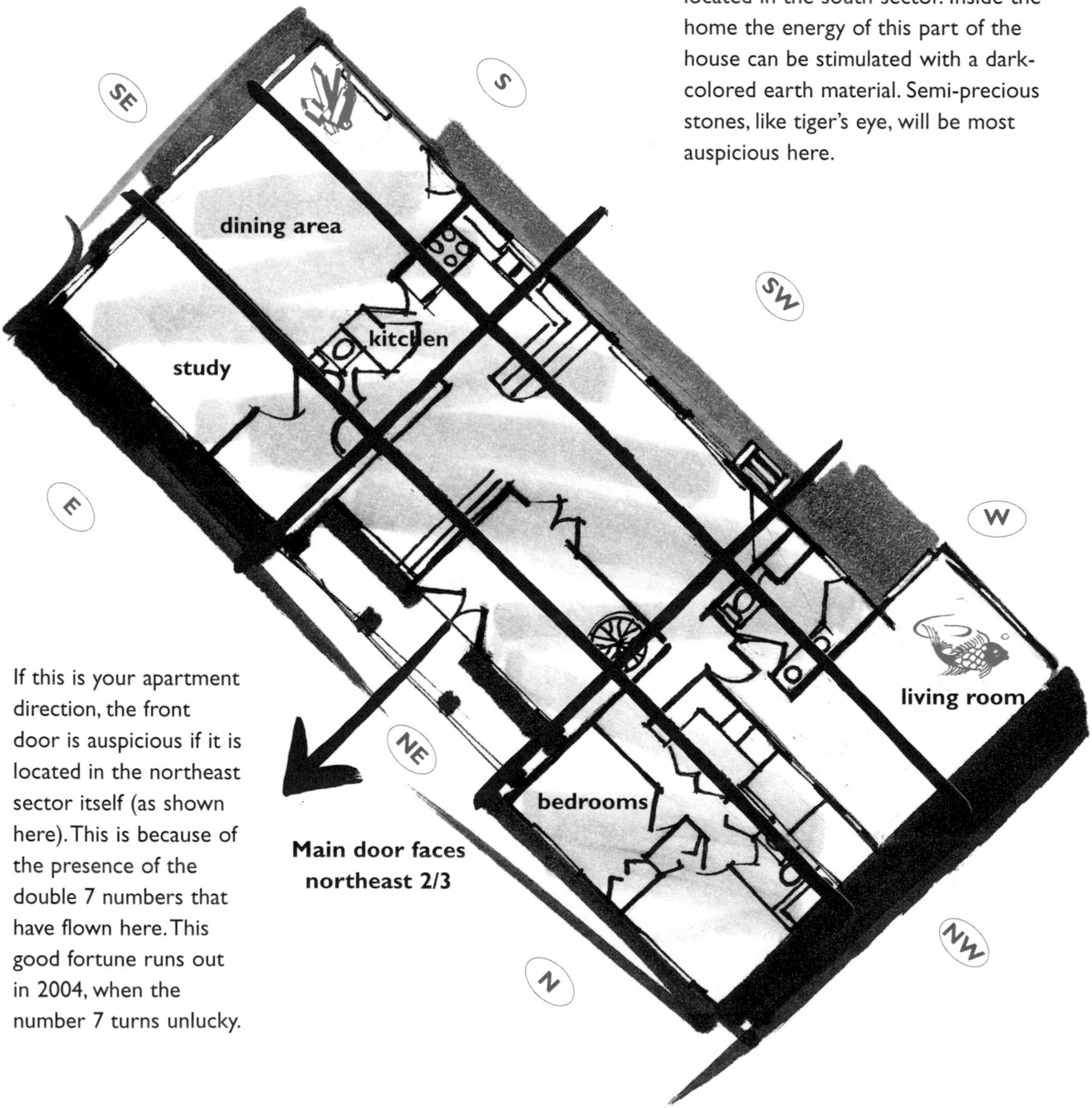

3 If this is your apartment direction, the front door is auspicious if it is located in the northeast sector itself (as shown here). This is because of the presence of the double 7 numbers that have flown here. This good fortune runs out in 2004, when the number 7 turns unlucky.

Main door faces northeast 2/3

A southwest 2/3-facing house (217.5 to 247.5°)

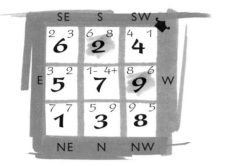

1 The water star 8 is located in the south. It will benefit the residents greatly if a water feature were to be built here. If it is placed outside, make sure there is a window or a door facing the water so that the good fortune chi is able to enter the home. If the water is placed inside the house, it can be in the south corner of the living room. Do not worry that this is the fire corner (south is fire). In this case, the water star brings money to the south!

2 The mountain star 8 is in the west. This corner also has an auspicious water star, so this corner is a very lucky part of the house. Anyone living here will benefit.

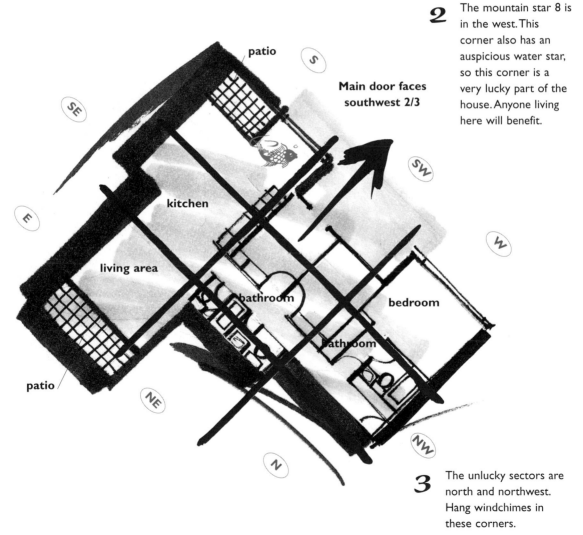

patio

Main door faces southwest 2/3

kitchen

living area

bathroom

bedroom

bathroom

patio

3 The unlucky sectors are north and northwest. Hang windchimes in these corners.

A southwest 1-facing house (202.5 to 217.5°) GROUND FLOOR

	SE	S	SW	
	9 5 **6**	5 9 **2**	7 7 **4**	
E	8 6 **5**	1+ 4- **7**	3 2 **9**	W
	4 1 **1**	6 8 **3**	2 3 **8**	
	NE	N	NW	

1 The water star 8 is located in the north. If this place is occupied by the bedroom one cannot activate water here, but in this house notice that the north is where the dining room is located – an excellent coincidence indeed. So if a water feature like a pond or waterfall were to be placed outside near the patio it would bring great wealth to the household. This is because the dining room is an important room. Moreover, there is an opening here (sliding French doors), thereby allowing the abundant water-activated chi to fly in. Upstairs the master bedroom is also located in this auspicious sector. These two features are sufficient to ensure the members of this household good fortune indeed.

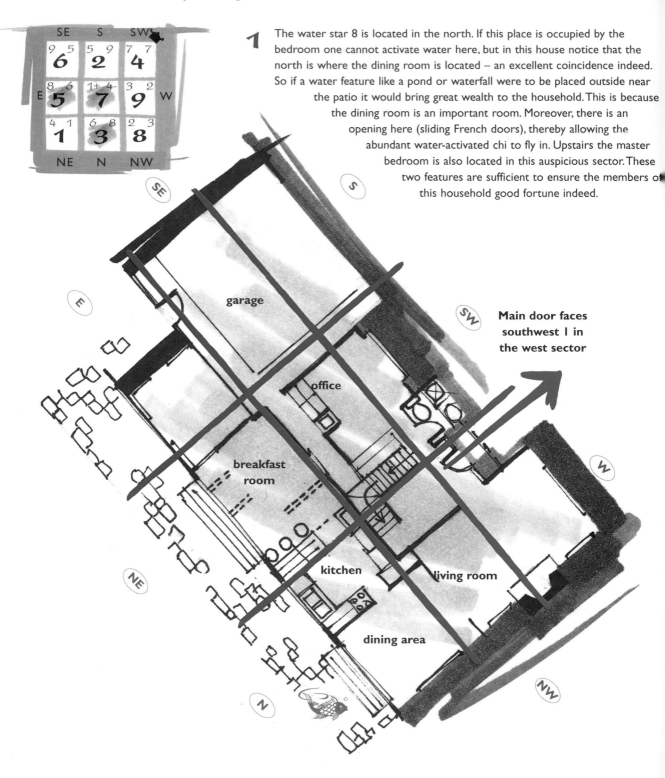

Main door faces southwest 1 in the west sector

garage

office

breakfast room

kitchen

living room

dining area

2 The mountain star 8 is located in the east, which is missing downstairs. Upstairs, it is in bedroom 2. Here it is a good idea to place a boulder or an amethyst geode tied with red string. This would bring a wonderful social life and good friends to the household. Perhaps on the ground level behind the garage there could be a stone garden. This would activate the mountain star very effectively.

3 The center numbers – 1,4,7 – form a special and magical combination, which brings enormous good fortune. Amongst period 7 houses only those facing southwest enjoy this fortunate occurrence. This is known as the *period string* combination and is regarded with great favor by many Feng Shui masters. If you are fortunate enough to have this combination of numbers, you will enjoy good Feng Shui for 180 years! The way to activate and take fullest advantage of this combination of numbers is to have a house with a large central room so that the influence of the numbers permeates the energy of the home. In this home the good thing is that the staircase is located here, which brings the chi upstairs. But the bathroom is also located in the center upstairs, thereby afflicting the good numbers.

bedroom 3

bedroom 2

bedroom 4

main bedroom

SE · S · SW · E · W · NE · N · NW

A southeast 1-facing house (112.5 to 127.5°)

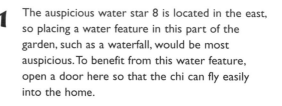

SE	S	SW
9 7 **6**	4 2 **2**	2 9 **4**
1 8 **5**	8- 6- **7**	6 4 **9**
5 3 **1**	3 1 **3**	7 5 **8**
NE	N	NW

E (left) — W (right)

1 The auspicious water star 8 is located in the east, so placing a water feature in this part of the garden, such as a waterfall, would be most auspicious. To benefit from this water feature, open a door here so that the chi can fly easily into the home.

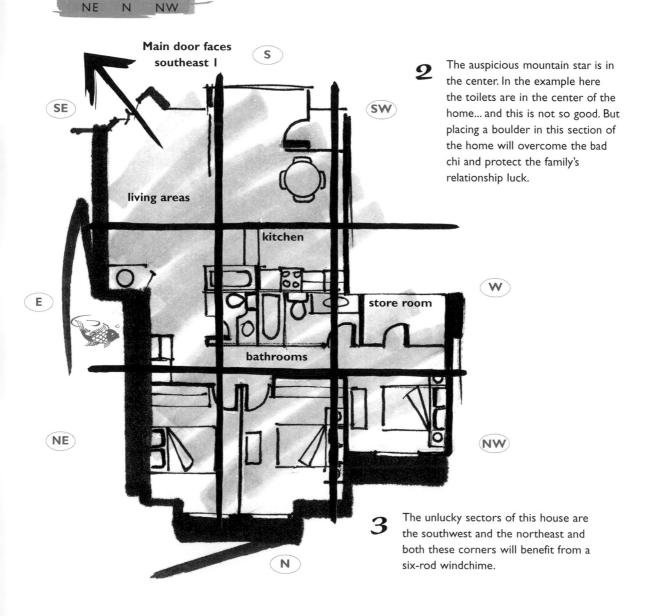

Main door faces southeast 1

S
SE
SW
living areas
kitchen
E
W
store room
bathrooms
NE
NW
N

2 The auspicious mountain star is in the center. In the example here the toilets are in the center of the home... and this is not so good. But placing a boulder in this section of the home will overcome the bad chi and protect the family's relationship luck.

3 The unlucky sectors of this house are the southwest and the northeast and both these corners will benefit from a six-rod windchime.

A southeast 2/3-facing house (127.5 to 157.5°)

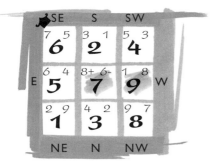

Main door faces southeast 2/3

1 The auspicious water star 8 is located in the west sector of the house. Unfortunately for this house, this sector is occupied by the kitchen, making it difficult to make the most of the auspicious water star. Here the solution is to place a water feature in the west sector of the large living area. This activates the small chi of the auspicious water star, and is usually equally effective.

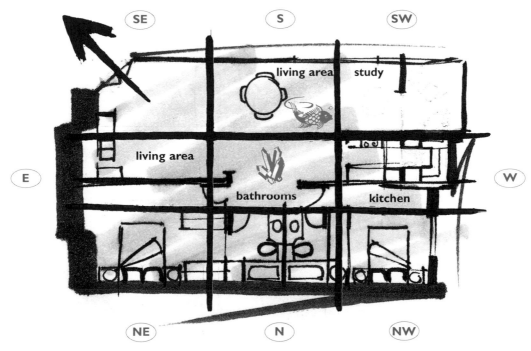

2 The auspicious mountain star 8 is located in the center of the home. If you place bright crystal lights here it will activate the strong earth energy needed to activate this auspicious earth element. 8 is the auspicious side of the earth element.

3 Unlucky sectors are the northeast and southwest corners of the home. The illness star is in the northeast and the accident star is in the southwest. In the northeast the bad star has been strengthened by the number 9. Place a metal five-rod windchime here to exhaust this bad energy. In the southwest there is also the fighting star 3, which causes lawsuits and problems.

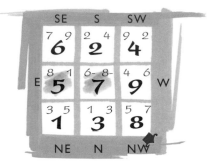

	SE	S	SW	
	7 9	2 4	9 2	
	6	**2**	**4**	
E	8 1	6- 8-	4 6	W
	5	**7**	**9**	
	3 5	1 3	5 7	
	1	**3**	**8**	
	NE	N	NW	

1 The lucky water star 8 is located in the center of the home where the kitchen is situated. This means that the energy of the kitchen afflicts the lucky 8 star number on the ground floor. Upstairs, the center is a hall. Once again, the lucky number 8 is not being put to use to enhance the luck of the residents. When you have lucky numbers in the center grid, the best way to take full advantage of it is to have a big hall in the center. This ensures that the good chi is felt over a large floor area of the home. It is not a bad idea to place an aquarium on the first floor, in the small hall which falls in the center of the house. This will activate the water star 8 upstairs and will enhance the luck of the house.

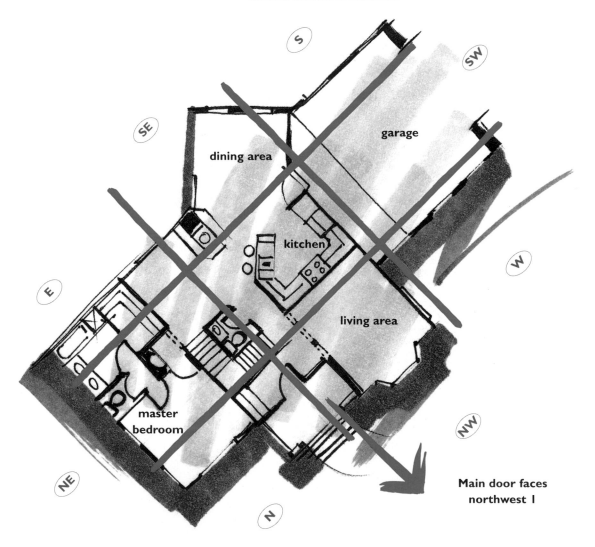

Main door faces
northwest 1

2 The lucky mountain star is located in the east sector grid of the house. On the ground floor this grid is half-missing – the reason for this is, of course, the protruding roof which has changed the dimensions of the natal chart, in effect creating a missing corner here. Upstairs, however, it is fine since the mountain star 8 falls squarely into bedroom 3. Anyone occupying this room will benefit. They will generally enjoy good relationships with everyone and if activated by a crystal or boulder, or anything made of earth materials, the good fortune from the mountain star 8 is considerably enhanced.

3 The southwest and northeast represent the unlucky axis of the house. To control the unlucky flying stars in these two sectors, hang a six-rod windchime. This will be very effective in exhausting the earth energies in these sectors.

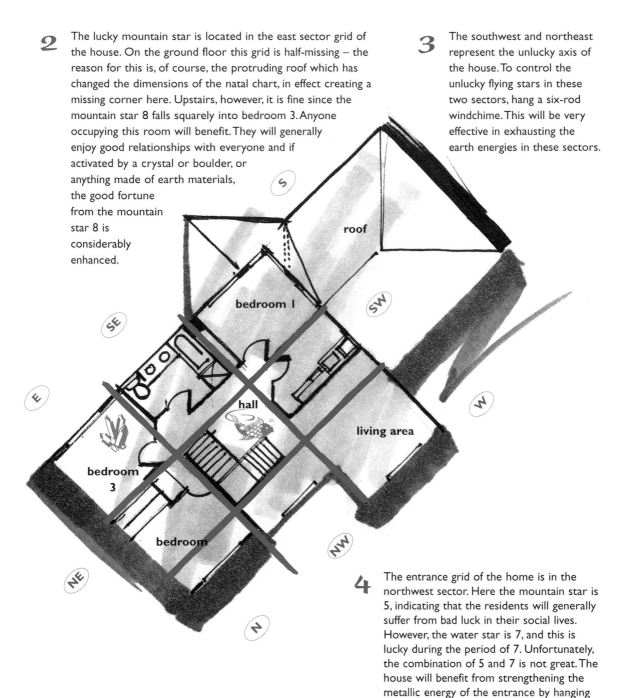

4 The entrance grid of the home is in the northwest sector. Here the mountain star is 5, indicating that the residents will generally suffer from bad luck in their social lives. However, the water star is 7, and this is lucky during the period of 7. Unfortunately, the combination of 5 and 7 is not great. The house will benefit from strengthening the metallic energy of the entrance by hanging coins and windchimes there.

A northwest 2/3-facing house   (307.5 to 337.5°)   **GROUND FLOOR**

1 The auspicious water star 8 has the kitchen in the center. Place an urn with yin water standing in the kitchen to reduce the effect of the kitchen. In the living area activate the small tai chi of the living room by placing an aquarium in the center part of the grid against the wall. This will bring good fortune to the living area. Upstairs the water star 8 seems to have flown to the sector housing the staircase and this is most auspicious, since it suggests good chi moving into the upper level of the home. Place a painting of fish on the staircase landing to activate the lucky water star.

This is the same house that we analyzed on the previous two pages, except it now has a door direction that faces northwest 2 instead of northwest 1. You will note that the mountain and water star numbers of all the sectors have changed, as have the luck sectors. This is the magic of flying star. By merely changing the door direction by a few degrees, sometimes the luck of the whole house can be affected.

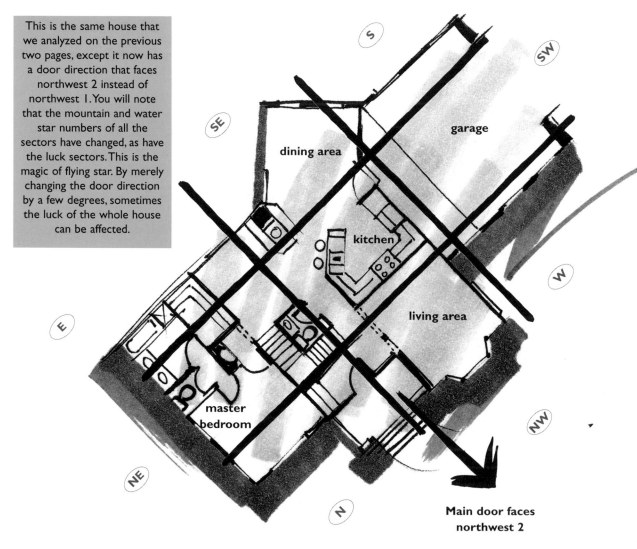

Main door faces northwest 2

2 The mountain star 8 of this house is located in the west sector, which is missing on both floors. This is a huge waste of good flying star chi, and shows that this house is better off with a different direction front door. The design of this house does not match the energy of its natal chart.

3 The unlucky sectors are the southwest and northeast corners of the home. Since the garage occupies the southwest, the affliction is not noticed. But the northeast is in part of the master bedroom. Here the numbers are 2 and 9, which bring serious illness. It is imperative that a six-rod all-metal windchime is hung here to safeguard the occupants from succumbing to a serious or fatal illness.

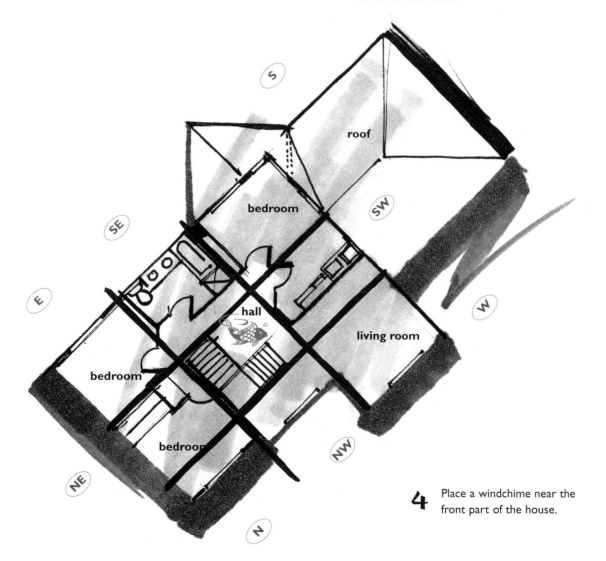

4 Place a windchime near the front part of the house.

conquering the
unlucky star
numbers

Knowing how to unlock the secrets of the lucky and unlucky star numbers will enable you to take remedial action when bad star numbers strike a particular part of your house. You will also be able to take advantage of times when auspicious stars bring you stunningly good luck.

The flight of the star numbers change and can be tracked annually, monthly, daily, and at hourly intervals, but it is not necessary to be so precise. However, you can use the Chinese Almanac (The Book of Auspicious Days) to keep track of the lucky and unlucky day and hour star numbers. I am happy enough to track just the month and annual unlucky stars. I believe that as long as we update the Feng Shui of the home each year by undertaking an annual assessment of the star numbers, the home is sufficiently safeguarded against any bad luck of that year.

When unlucky annual and monthly stars occur together in any of the nine-sector grids in the natal chart, exceptional bad luck can occur while these flying numbers are in residence. What this means is that if, for example, your bedroom happens to be located in that part of the house, then you could meet up with some kind of misfortune or loss. How serious this misfortune turns out to be depends on two other factors.

1 If the star numbers on your natal chart are inauspicious and the unlucky numbers also occur in your particular corner, the potential for serious misfortune is multiplied a hundredfold. To alleviate this increased potential for misfortune, you must either vacate your room by going on holiday or preferably, move to another part of the house until the month is over.

2 It also depends on the steps you take to dissolve or reduce the effect of these flying numbers. Different star numbers require different remedies or antidotes, and knowing this is what counts as Feng Shui magic. Often the cure is quite simple, and may use the theory of the five elements to overcome particular unlucky numbers. Alternatively, it may be based on which sector of the house is being afflicted by the unlucky numbers, as different corners of the home represent different element attributes.

The effect of unlucky or harmful flying numbers can be overcome with correct Feng Shui counter measures, but before doing this you need to work out where the bad corners are in each year, and each month.

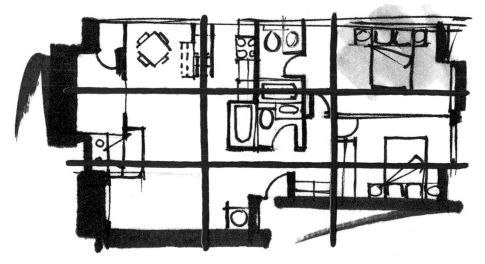

Use the flying star natal charts to check out the location of monthly and annual bad flying stars. Then you can avoid bad fortune, particularly if the bad stars affect areas of the home in which you spend lots of time, such as the bedroom.

Feng Shui alchemists are quite relaxed when only the year star or the month star is bad, but when both the year and month stars are bad, then we will need to be more careful.

annual star
numbers to look out for

When the unlucky stars 5, 3, 2 and, after February 4, 2004, 7, combine with each other, any bad luck is compounded and the effect multiplied. If either 2 or 5 are combined with the number 9, the bad chi is multiplied even more. In addition, the number 5 is so unlucky that a special section has been devoted to explaining and overcoming its bad effect.

The special chart given here reveals which sectors are affected each year over a nine-year cycle, which then repeats itself so that whatever sector is afflicted in 2001 will be similarly afflicted in 2010.

As Feng Shui is dynamic, you should update your Feng Shui annually. Keep this chart carefully, as it contains the information you need to identify the afflicted sectors of your home. Once you know which sectors are afflicted, you will be able to place special antidotes to cure them. If it is difficult to install these cures, or you cannot find them, you

Cures for monthly and annual flying star afflictions are easy to install. In sectors where the illness star 2 or the deadly star 5 fly in, hang a six-rod all-metal windchime (when the affliction hits south, southwest, and northeast) in the corner afflicted. Use a five-rod all-metal windchime for other sectors. Sectors afflicted by the quarrelsome star 3 can be remedied by the placement of an urn of still, cool yin water. It will absorb all the chi of misunderstandings, ensuring domestic peace. Sectors that are affected by the number 7 could begin to feel the evil influence of this star number as we are fast approaching the changeover to period 8. It is advisable to place a small lamp to control the ill effects of this number when it appears in any sector.

should avoid sleeping or working in the affected sectors. The affliction lasts for a month if it is caused by the month star, and for a year if the annual star number is the cause.

Placing still, yin water in sectors afflicted by the quarrelsome star number 3 absorbs the stars negative influences.

Sectors afflicted by annual stars 2001–2009

HSIA YEAR*	Grave Misfortune Star 5	Serious Illness Star 2	Quarrelsome Star 3	Violence Star 7**
2001	Southwest	Northeast	South	Brings good luck
2002	East	South	North	Brings good luck
2003	Southeast	North	Southwest	Brings good luck
2004	Center	Southwest	East	West
2005	Northwest	East	Southeast	Northeast
2006	West	Southeast	Center	South
2007	Northeast	Center	Northwest	North
2008	South	Northwest	West	Southwest
2009	North	West	Northeast	East

* The years here refer to the Chinese calendar years which start of February 4 of each equivalent western calendar year. This is based, therefore, on the Hsia calendar rather than the lunar calendar.
** The number 7 brings good luck up to the end of 2003, and severe bad luck from 2004.

lo shu squares

Once you know the Lo Shu reigning number for the year, you can use the Lo Shu charts to identify the good and bad sectors of your home. Note the compass sector where the good and bad luck numbers are placed. The reigning number is always placed in the center, and you will see that the star numbers "fly" around the grid and always in the same sequence. For annual Lo Shu Squares, the center number moves in a descending sequence from 9 to 8 to 7, and so on. The monthly numbers also move in a descending sequence.

The Lo Shu Squares of each of the nine years, 2001–2009.

	SE	S	SW	
	7	3	5	
E	6	8	1	W
	2	4	9	
	NE	N	NW	

2001

	SE	S	SW	
	6	2	4	
E	5	7	9	W
	1	3	8	
	NE	N	NW	

2002

	SE	S	SW	
	5	1	3	
E	4	6	8	W
	9	2	7	
	NE	N	NW	

2003

	SE	S	SW	
	4	9	2	
E	3	5	7	W
	8	1	6	
	NE	N	NW	

2004

	SE	S	SW	
	3	8	1	
E	2	4	6	W
	7	9	5	
	NE	N	NW	

2005

	SE	S	SW	
	2	7	9	
E	1	3	5	W
	6	8	4	
	NE	N	NW	

2006

	SE	S	SW	
	1	6	8	
E	9	2	4	W
	5	7	3	
	NE	N	NW	

2007

	SE	S	SW	
	9	5	7	
E	8	1	3	W
	4	6	2	
	NE	N	NW	

2008

	SE	S	SW	
	8	4	6	
E	7	9	2	W
	3	5	1	
	NE	N	NW	

2009

Reigning Lo Shu numbers 1998 to 2023

YEAR	Reigning Lo Shu number	YEAR	Reigning Lo Shu number
1998	2	2011	7
1999	1	2012	6
2000	9	2013	5
2001	8	2014	4
2002	7	2015	3
2003	6	2016	2
2004	5	2017	1
2005	4	2018	9
2006	3	2019	8
2007	2	2020	7
2008	1	2021	6
2009	9	2022	5
2010	8	2023	4

The reigning Lo Shu number is the *center* number of the Lo Shu grid. So to obtain the grid for each year simply check the center number, and then match it with the relevant grid shown on the previous page.

Auspicious annual stars 2001 to 2009

HSIA YEAR	Auspicious White Earth star 8 is in the	Auspicious White Heaven star 6 is in the	Auspicious White Water Element star 1 is in the	Auspicious Green Wood star 4 is in the
2001	Center	East	West	North
2002	Northwest	Southeast	Northeast	Southwest
2003	West	Center	South	East
2004	Northeast	Northwest	North	Southeast
2005	South	West	Southwest	Center
2006	North	Northeast	East	Northwest
2007	Southwest	South	Southeast	West
2008	East	North	Center	Northeast
2009	Southeast	Southwest	Northwest	South

The 8 star brings wealth, prosperity, and lots of money luck
The 6 star brings luck from heaven with plenty of success and helpful people
The 1 star brings career luck in promotions and recognition if your bedroom enjoys this star
The 4 star brings literary luck and also the luck of love, unless afflicted by excessive water.

overcoming the monthly
bad stars

In addition to the annual star numbers, you should fine-tune your practice of numerology magic in Feng Shui by undertaking a monthly analysis. According to the Chinese calendar there are twelve months in a year, and sometimes thirteen months. Unless you know the monthly analysis of the star numbers, you will not be able to pinpoint when the bad luck of afflicted sectors is compounded by the monthly afflictions and reaches its peak. This will affect your ability to practice this powerful technique and avert misfortune.

To undertake the monthly analysis you need to work with the Lo Shu squares again, and also refer to the summary of the Hsia monthly calendar given opposite, which shows you two important things. Firstly it shows the western equivalent starting dates for each of the Chinese months and, secondly, it shows the reigning Lo Shu numbers for that month. You can see from the chart that this reigning number depends on which animal sign is ruling in that year.

Using these charts you will see, for example, that in the year of the Horse (2002) the ruling Lo Shu number for the second month is 7. To know which sector is afflicted by the unlucky number 5 star in that second month you refer to the Lo Shu Square with 7 in the center and then look for the afflicted number 5. You will see that in the second Chinese month of the year of the Horse, the unlucky afflicted sector is east, which also has the annual 5. So the east is particularly dangerous for everyone in that month.

Summary of the Hsia monthly calendar

Equivalent starting date of the CHINESE SOLAR MONTH (western calendar date)	THE CHINESE MONTH (the solar months of the Chinese calendar)	Lo Shu reigning number in the year of the Rat, Rabbit, Horse, & Rooster	Lo Shu reigning number in the year of the Dog, Dragon, Ox, & Sheep	Lo Shu reigning number in the year of the Tiger, Pig, Snake, & Monkey
February 4	month 1	8	5	2
March 6	month 2	7	4	1
April 5	month 3	6	3	9
May 6	month 4	5	2	8
June 6	month 5	4	1	7
July 7	month 6	3	9	6
August 8	month 7	2	8	5
September 8	month 8	1	7	4
October 8	month 9	9	6	3
November 7	month 10	8	5	2
December 7	month 11	7	4	1
January 6	month 12	6	3	9

The dates on the first column may have a variation of one day plus or minus, depending on the year.

installing
feng shui cures

You will need to install Feng Shui cures in the rooms within the compass sectors afflicted by the 5, the 2, the 3, (and after 2004) the 7 stars, especially when both the annual and monthly stars cause these afflictions.

Full concentration of the mind is what brings success. No matter how simple the practice has been made for you, you must concentrate and pay attention to what you are doing. I always make sure I am well rested before I undertake any kind of serious Feng Shui practice. It is even better if you know how to meditate, to still the mind and allow yourself to enter into a state of relaxed, but very focused, concentration. That is when your mental powers are at their best. You will then be practicing Feng Shui at two dimensions of consciousness, the inner and the outer levels.

There are old Chinese texts devoted exclusively to overcoming the intangible bad luck brought by star numbers every year. The cures that I give I have tried myself over a period of many years to assure myself that they turnaround bad luck, and I have been astounded by their effectiveness. It is on this basis that these cures have been recommended.

Ideally I prefer to incorporate these Feng Shui cures and also the energizers into decorative objects that look good in a modern home.

It is important to focus your intent on what you want Feng Shui to do for you. Meditating upon your wishes, always with pure motives, is an excellent way to prepare yourself before you begin.

While I do like the traditional Chinese versions of these cures I have discovered that it is not the esoteric aspect of the symbols that makes them work, but rather the combination of postures, directions, numbers, colors, and dimensions, and most importantly the materials used that make symbolic cures particularly effective.

> Alchemy requires objects to be made of metal compounds and mixes of colors which makes metal cures the most effective, especially for overcoming the afflicting stars 5 and 2.

In addition, Feng Shui cures work better when placed during auspicious days and auspicious hours of the day. These can be easily checked if you have the Chinese Almanac, or you can access the wofs.com website, which carries a very comprehensive and useful Almanac service free of charge.

There is also a correct way and an incorrect way of installing feng shui cures, depending on what cures are being used. Some cures, like the placement of windchimes, can be positioned so wrongly that they can cause accidents to manifest. There are therefore do's and don'ts related to each of the cures. So please do read the section on cures carefully!

Special attention should also be devoted to the display of Feng Shui enhancers. Use these enhancers in a clever way so there is balance and harmony created. They should also look good. If your karma or heaven luck is good, enhancers work very fast, and you would feel instinctively good about them. If you are going through a bad astrological period it is possible that you could place them incorrectly, and then they do little to attract good luck.

making mistakes
and the quick fix

It is very important to use a good compass to accurately determine the direction of your home. Estimating the direction according to where the sun rises or sets leads to mistakes. It is not recommended.

Another common cause for mistakes is when you mix methods. It is simply not possible to do this, even for Feng Shui consultants. This causes confusion and neither method works. I strongly discourage this.

Such mistakes usually happen when you attend Feng Shui courses from different masters who each use a different method. I know of students who pride themselves on being very advanced because they learn from an old master who is teaching them yin Feng Shui. They think that this is very advanced Feng Shui, and it is. But it does not apply to yang dwellings: the houses of the living. This type of feng shui applies to grave sites and another dimension of existence altogether, which is why I call it yin Feng Shui. Attempts to use yin Feng Shui formulas to second-guess Feng Shui cures for yang dwellings simply will not work.

The methods in this book enable you to practice the Feng Shui of the Three Period, also known as Flying Star Numbers Feng Shui. The analysis, practices, cures, and enhancers apply only for the houses of the living, the yang dwelling houses. They will work, seemingly like magic. The scale of success depends on your own heaven and mankind luck. Feng Shui is earth luck. It is a powerful component of the trinity of luck, so practice it with confidence and a good motive. The Flying Star natal charts enable you to determine good and bad luck sectors accurately, and the chapters on cures and enhancers will improve your home Feng Shui.

The Quick Fix

Even if you do nothing else, you will enjoy good money luck by simply activating the water star 8 of your natal chart, and good relationship luck by energizing the mountain star 8.

The water star 8 is activated when there is the presence of yang water or other water features (see Tip 12 and Tip 8), while the mountain star is energized by building a mountain of gold, or simply by placing a large natural crystal geode or boulder in the sector.

The other aspect of the quick fix is to avoid sleeping, working, and living in a space that is afflicted by unlucky stars. The easiest way is simply to move out of any space that has the afflicted annual and monthly stars 5 or 2, which also show up in the natal charts. When more than two fives/twos are in the same sector the bad luck is very severe. Alternatively, you can hang a six-rod windchime in these areas. You will learn how to get the best from your windchimes in Tip 23.

A natural crystal geode and a symbolic "mountain of gold" activates the lucky mountain star in flying star Feng Shui.

overcoming the
illness stars

At certain times, the illness star 2 and deadly star 5 congregate and fly into a compass sector which also has the 2 and 5 as the water or mountain star, or as the main star numeral. This is a particularly unfortunate combination with a direct and negative affect on health. When these stars afflict the garage or a store room, however, its negative effect is said to be dispersed or "locked up."

When you know which sector of your house has the illness stars you should check if there are bedrooms in these afflicted sectors. If so, then something should be done immediately. Do not wait for the annual and monthly 2s and 5s to come in at the same time. Moving out of the afflicted room that month will enable you to conquer the illness star, but if you cannot keep the room empty while this sector is afflicted, use one

- Hang six-rod, all-metal windchimes that are large and hollow, placing them at body level against one of the walls. Never hang windchimes high above, from the ceiling. If the windchimes can be made to create metallic sounds, the potency of the windchime is enhanced, but if there is no breeze you can strengthen the metal energy by hanging two similar windchimes, on opposite walls and facing each other.

- Place a large metallic bell in the sector that is afflicted. Preferably the bell should be a singing bell that is made of seven types of metal incorporating the seven planets and the seven energy points of your body (see Tip 24). These bells are best used as energizers, but they are also extremely effective in exhausting the severely afflicted earth energy of 2s and 5s.

of two effective cures to combat the illness stars 2 or 5. Both methods require the use of strong metal energy.

The following table shows where the danger illness sectors are during period 7. You can compare this table against the sixteen natal charts on pages 125–145, and then work out which of those houses have rooms afflicted by illness stars.

The location of illness sectors for period 7 (1984–2004)

HOUSE CATEGORY	MAIN STAR 2 **	MAIN STAR 5**	WATER STAR 2	MOUNTAIN STAR 2	WATER STAR 5	MOUNTAIN STAR 5
East 1	South	East	Southwest	West	Center	North
East 2/3 *	South *	East	Northeast	East	Center	South *
North 1	South	East	Southeast	Center	West	Southwest
North 2/3 *	South	East *	Northwest	Center	East *	Northeast
South 1	South	East	Center	Southeast	Southwest	West
South 2/3 *	South	East *	Center	Northwest	Northeast	East *
Northeast 1 *	South *	East	Northwest	West	South *	Southeast
Northeast 2/3	South	East	Southeast	East	North	Northwest
Northwest 1 *	South	East	Southwest	South *	Northeast	Northwest
Northwest 2/3	South	East	Northeast	North	Southwest	Southeast
Southeast 1	South	East	South *	Southwest	Northwest	Northeast
Southeast 2/3	South	East	North	Northeast	Southeast	Southwest
Southwest 1*	South	East	West	Northwest	Southeast	South *
Southwest 2/3*	South	East	East *	Southeast	Northwest	North
West 1	South	East	West	Southwest	North	Center
West 2/3 **	South	East	East *	Northeast	South *	Center

** The table refers only to current period of 7 house natal charts. So the main star numbers for all the charts will be the same. So in this period of 7 residents occupying bedrooms located in the east and south must watch out when the annual and monthly 2s and 5s come in together as these will trigger the illness chi. The answer is to use six-rod windchimes.

* Houses where the illness stars can pose an obvious threat. Note that if the afflicted sectors fall within the garage or in "missing corners" of your home, they cannot harm residents.

Redecorating the home always brings in fresh energy that revitalizes and rejuvenates. Regular home maintenance that requires a certain amount of renovation activates the chi of the space, forcing stagnating chi to be swept out of its hiding places, and stale chi to evaporate. So it is excellent to redecorate your home on a regular basis, preferably every two or three years, but if this is not possible, then at least move the furniture around and introduce one new item while discarding something old and worn out. This replacement of something old with something new provides the catalyst for energy to shift and move.

Chinese alchemy always begins with the correct hour and the correct orientation, and your success depends on these two basic factors. When you respect these guidelines, changing the energy of your interiors will bring you brand-new opportunities for success. Luck flies through your door and into your home. You and all who live within your home will feel completely recharged.

seven

redecorating magic

start renovations
auspiciously

When you renovate your home it is important to select an auspicious start date to ensure that construction work begins and ends in those parts of the home that have good luck star numbers. It is important to work out which corners of the home must not be disturbed to avoid causing afflicted energy to multiply.

Spring cleaning the space to be renovated, boxing up your "treasures," and generally clearing the air will bring in new energy. Clearing and discarding, sorting, and boxing allows stale chi which has turned yin and lifeless to dissolve. It also allows fresh new chi to come into the home. With curtains and drapes, merely taking them down to be washed creates brand new energy for the room. Cleanliness plays a big role in Feng Shui!

Always do this clearing chore with at least one window open and if possible let the sunlight in. This provides an escape route for old, tired chi to fly out of your house, and for new yang-activated chi to fly in.

Selecting an Auspicious Day to Begin

The Chinese always use the Almanac or Book of Auspicious Days to select the correct day and hour to start any kind of construction or demolition work on homes and buildings. It categorizes both the Chinese lunar days and the equivalent English calendar days, offering the entire spectrum of good and bad days and hours for undertaking a broad variety of activities.

If you cannot find an Almanac, follow a simple rule that auspicious days are on the first day of the first lunar month, the second day of the

second lunar month, the third day of the third lunar month and so on, until you reach the twelfth month. The first and fifteenth days of lunar months are also said to be auspicious, especially the fifteenth, since that is when the moon is at its brightest. From this it is clear that the first half of the month, when the moon is waxing, is preferred for activating the energy of the home, for this is what renovation work involves.

Selecting the Most Auspicious Hour

Selecting an auspicious time of the day to begin is simple with an Almanac, but generally between 7am and 11am is safe to start work. Check that the hour is auspicious for you, based on your animal sign, and also that it does not conflict with any member of your family. If it does then just make sure that person is not present when renovation work begins.

Hours of the day based on animal signs
(check the calendar on page 200–203 to find out your animal sign)

HOURS OF THE DAY		AUSPICIOUS for...	IN CONFLICT with...	Polarity & element
Zi	11pm to 1am	rat	horse	yang water
Chou	1am to 3am	ox	sheep	yin earth
Yin	3am to 5am	tiger	monkey	yang wood
Mao	5am to 7am	rabbit	rooster	yin wood
Chen	7am to 9am	dragon	dog	yang earth
Si	9am to 11am	snake	pig	yin fire
Wu	11am to 1pm	horse	rat	yang fire
Wei	1pm to 3pm	sheep	ox	yin earth
Shen	3pm to 5pm	monkey	tiger	yang metal
You	5pm to 7pm	rooster	rabbit	yin metal
Xi	7pm to 9pm	dog	dragon	yang earth
Hai	9pm to 11pm	pig	snake	yin water

watching out for the
three killings

When you undertake any kind of redecorating work it is imperative that you do not inadvertently activate the *sarm saat*, known as the Three Killings. The effect of this is to bring three types of bad luck – sickness, financial loss, and accidents. The sector of the house occupied by the three killings is always dangerous and it changes from year to year. The affliction is activated by simply digging a hole or banging and knocking in that part of the house. It is therefore important to find out where the three killings resides each year and avoid activities that energize it.

The Locations of the Three Killings

Each year the three killings flies from one cardinal direction to the next and occupies a full 90 degrees of the compass. Hence:

In the years of the	OX, ROOSTER, and SNAKE	the location is	East
In the years of the	BOAR, RABBIT, and SHEEP	the location is	West
In the years of the	MONKEY, RAT, and DRAGON	the location is	South
In the years of the	DOG, HORSE, and TIGER	the location is	North

So in the year 2001, the year of the Snake, the three killings reside in the east, and in 2002, during the year of the Horse, the three killings reside in the north.

The two useful rules to follow regarding the three killings are firstly never to have the three killings behind you. It is more advantageous to confront it. Thus, when it is in the west, you should sit facing the west rather than east, with the west behind you. When the three killings is behind you, it "kills" you. Secondly, house repairs and renovations may be undertaken in

locations opposite but not in the location housing the three killings. This is because when you directly confront the three killings you can overcome it, but if you disturb it in its own domain, you are seriously asking for trouble! So, in 2002 you really should not undertake any renovations in the north sector of your house.

If for some reason you absolutely have to undertake renovations in the north part of your home in the year 2002, then it is necessary to do the following:

1 Appease the three killings palace in the north by making a food offering to the land spirits. Place a plate of biscuits on the floor where the three killings reside.

2 Be sure to conduct the official starting ceremony in another sector that is not afflicted by other bad annual stars. Start with a symbolic loud announcement together with one big hit with the drill and then work your way to the north, and then on to another sector. *Never* begin work in the place of the three killings, and do not complete the renovation there either, but choose an auspicious corner in which to end.

Always sit so you confront the sector of your home or office that is occupied by the three killings. This weakens its destructive influence.

3 Placing the image of the Laughing Buddha in the sector where the three killings is located is an excellent antidote. The Buddha has the power to sweep all troubles he encounters into his bag, thereby transforming them into happiness.

getting support from the
grand duke

If the Grand Duke Jupiter has been disturbed or offended by renovations in his sector of your home, place the dragon-dog Pi Yao there to appease him.

One of the most stringent guidelines about renovations is that the Palace of the *Tai Sui*, popularly known as the Grand Duke Jupiter, must not be disturbed or confronted. This will incur his wrath and the consequences are said to be most dire. It is for this reason that each new year the first thing Feng Shui masters in Hong Kong do is calculate the Grand Duke's location and identify it for their clients. When the Grand Duke is honored, the family receives his support and good fortune. So the Chinese are very sensitive to the Grand Duke's presence, and treat him with respect. Like the Three Killings, his location changes every year, so you should find out where he resides each year.

The good news, however, is that the Grand Duke occupies only fifteen degrees of the compass, so it is easy to avoid offending him.

The rules to observe are:

1 Firstly, you should never confront the Grand Duke by sitting in a position that is directly facing him. For example, in 2001, the year of the Snake, the Grand Duke resides in the south-southeast sector of your home. This means you should not sit north-northwest facing south-southeast. No matter how auspicious facing south or southeast may be for you personally, you must strenuously guard against doing this in all cases.

2 Secondly, never incur the Grand Duke's wrath by disturbing him. This means that you should never undertake any renovation or construction works in the sector where he resides. Use a good compass to determine this, and superimpose the nine-sector Lo Shu grid to help you demarcate this entire sector. If your plans involve construction work in parts of your home or office, do be certain not to touch this sector at all. Wait for the following year. If in doubt, it is better to postpone your plans!

3 If you have already inadvertently disturbed the Grand Duke's palace, the most effective way to appease him is to place a Pi Yao image in the corner afflicted. Do this immediately to avoid misfortune. It is interesting to note that ancient Chinese warlords would not advance into battle in the direction of the Grand Duke. They always made sure he was behind them.

The Locations of the Grand Duke

Lunar year – (beginning on Feb. 4 each year)	Ruling animal sign (those born under this sign are said to disturb the Grand Duke)	The animal sign said to be in direct conflict with the Grand Duke. Bad luck!	The location of the palace of the Grand Duke Jupiter (15 degrees). Do not disturb this corner
2001	SNAKE	BOAR	South–southeast
2002	HORSE	RAT	South
2003	SHEEP	OX	South–southwest
2004	MONKEY	TIGER	West–southwest
2005	ROOSTER	RABBIT	West
2006	DOG	DRAGON	West–northwest
2007	BOAR	SNAKE	North–northwest
2008	RAT	HORSE	North
2009	OX	SHEEP	North–northeast
2010	TIGER	MONKEY	East–northeast
2011	RABBIT	ROOSTER	East
2012	DRAGON	DOG	East–southeast

watching out for the deadly
five yellow

You must watch out for the terrible results that can come from unwittingly activating the deadly Five Yellow star (known as the *wu wang*) by undertaking renovations in the part of the home occupied by the Five Yellow during a particular month or year. This is of paramount importance and note that in some years he is more terrible than in others.

The Five Yellow is a configuration of intangible forces that is extremely inauspicious when it enters a particular sector under the yearly Lo Shu grid. The Five Yellow occupies a square in this imaginary grid and his palace takes up 45 compass degrees.

Offer three cups of wine, fruit, and rice to the earth spirits before embarking on renovation work.

When the Five Yellow is in residence, any renovation work in that sector will create problems for the household. It is a good idea to hang one or several six-rod windchimes to press down on the bad luck created by the Five Yellow in the sector where it appears. Its location for the next 100 years is presented in the table opposite.

The Ritual of Starting Renovation Work

Having selected the day and the hour you must also find the most auspicious corner to start the work in order not to disturb the unlucky flying stars – the Three Killings, the Grand Duke, or the Five Yellow. To ensure trouble-free work it is worthwhile observing this small ritual. Ask the main contractor to show up at the appointed hour with a digging tool, a saw, or a drill. Any one of these implements is sufficient. Then spread out a small mini-feast of three cups of wine, a plate of fruit, and a bowl of rice or biscuits. These offerings are to the earth spirits occupying the space in your home, officially informing them that there will be some disturbance to their space for a short period. If possible, specify the estimated time it will take. Then request their indulgence for disturbing their space. Offer the feast as a peace offering. Then tell the contractor to symbolically dig or drill, and say very loudly, "We are now commencing the renovation work of this house," quoting the address of the house. Announce this three times.

And that is all there is to it. If the contractor finds that day convenient, he can then proceed. If he is not ready, it doesn't matter if he begins on another day as officially he is said to have begun work. Meanwhile, the food offering should be left for 24 hours and then thrown away. If you taste the food you will find that it has lost most of its taste and will now appear bland! If you eat the food you could get mouth ulcers!

In the following lunar years, the Five Yellow is located as follows:

Years	Five Yellow Location
1999, 2008, 2017, 2026, 2035, 2044, 2053, 2062, 2071, 2080, and 2089	in the south
2007, 2016, 2025, 2034, 2043, 2052, 2061, 2070, 2079, 2088, and 2097	in the northeast
2006, 2015, 2024, 2033, 2042, 2051, 2060, 2069, 2078, 2087, and 2096	in the west
2005, 2014, 2023, 2032, 2041, 2050, 2059, 2068, 2077, 2086, and 2095	in the northwest
2004, 2013, 2022, 2031, 2040, 2049, 2058, 2067, 2076, 2085, and 2094	in the center
2003, 2012, 2021, 2030, 2039, 2048, 2057, 2066, 2076, 2084, and 2093	in the southeast
2002, 2011, 2020, 2029, 2038, 2047, 2056, 2065, 2074, 2083, and 2092	in the east
2001, 2010, 2019, 2028, 2037, 2046, 2055, 2064, 2073, 2082, and 2091	in the southwest
2000, 2009, 2018, 2027, 2036, 2045, 2054, 2063, 2072, 2081, and 2090	in the north

check if your chi energy harmonizes with you home

A popular method of Feng Shui widely used by practitioners is to work out whether the intangible energy of each home is synchronized or in harmony with the energy of the residents. This involves the matching of two easy formulas, which then reveal whether or not a home will be auspicious for you.

This is a simple compass formula method that is an amalgamation of the Eight Mansions and Flying Star methods of Compass Feng Shui. I find this method useful to countercheck the lucky and unlucky sectors of any house based on the annual stars, and on the individuals based on their respective KUA numbers.

The KUA number enables anyone to determine the following:
- Their four auspicious directions – for success, health, romance, and personal development
- Their four unlucky directions – brought by bad luck, five ghosts, six killings, and total loss
- Their personalized Feng Shui auspicious element
- Their personalized Feng Shui trigram
- Their Lo shu number and Lo Shu square

The four auspicious directions are: Sheng Chi (generating breath), Tien Yi (doctor from heaven), Nien Yen (longevity with rich descendants), and Fu Wei (overall harmony). The four inauspicious directions are: Ho Hai (accidents and mishaps), Lui Sha (six killings), Wu Kwei (five ghosts), and Chueh Ming (total loss of descendants).

From these derivatives, you can compare your KUA attributes against those of your home, and then determine if the chi forces of your home are compatible with your personalized chi forces. However, while the KUA number gives you your personalized attributes, it is what is called the *sitting direction* of the home that gives your home its Feng Shui attributes. Note that those living in apartments have to use the sitting direction of the whole building in order to determine the Feng Shui attributes of their apartment.

The KUA Number

To determine your KUA number, lyou need your Chinese year of birth – this is based on the Chinese Hsia calendar*. For ease of reference use February 4 as the start of the Chinese year, instead of January 1, which is based on the western calendar. So if you were born before February 4 of your year of birth, deduct one from your year of birth in the calculation of your KUA number given below.

Armed with your KUA number, you can investigate whether your existing house or apartment building is compatible with your KUA

*Note that the Hsia calendar differs from the lunar calendar, whose new year date varies from year to year. Generally KUA numbers are based on the lunar calendar. However, certain Feng Shui masters also use the Hsia calendar which starts the year at the beginning of the spring which is February 4.

How to calculate your KUA number

- Add the last two digits of your Chinese year of birth e.g. for 1944, add 4 + 4 = 8
- If this sum has two digits, reduce it to a single digit e.g. 1979 so 7 + 9 =16; then 1 + 6 = 7
- For men deduct the result from 10, so for those born in 1944, it will be 10 − 8 = 2. Thus, the KUA number is 2. And for those born in 1979 their KUA number is 10 − 7 = 3
- For women add 5, so for women born in 1944 the equation is 4 + 4 = 8 + 5 = 13; then 1 + 3 = 4 so the KUA number is 4, while for women born in 1979 their KUA number is 7 + 9 = 16, add 1 + 6 = 7 + 5 = 12, then add 1 + 2 = 3

number and thus with you. Every house holds different luck for different people based on the compatibility of the Feng Shui intangible forces associated with different houses and different individuals.

At the same time, not all houses have the same degree of luck for everyone. The analysis is based on the eight main directions of the compass, and the KUA formula divides these four directions into east group directions and west group directions.

In the same way, individuals are also divided into east-group people and west-group people. To discover if you are east or west group, and exactly what each direction means for you, refer to the chart given below.

The chart opposite reveals the extent of compatibility of houses to individuals. This is based on the sitting direction of the house, which is

KUA numbers and directions

Meaning of direction	KUA Number									
	1 East	2 West	3 East	4 East	5 West Men	5 West Women	6 West	7 West	8 West	9 East
Personal Growth	N	SW	E	SE	SW	NE	NW	W	NE	S
Success	SE	NE	S	N	NE	SW	W	NW	SW	E
Health	E	W	N	S	W	NW	NE	SW	NW	SE
Romance	S	NW	SE	E	NW	W	SW	NE	W	N
Bad luck	W	E	SW	NW	E	S	SE	N	S	NE
Five Ghosts	NE	SE	NW	SW	SE	N	E	S	N	W
Six Killings	NW	S	NE	W	S	E	N	SE	E	SW
Total Loss	SW	N	W	NE	N	SE	S	E	SE	NW

The west-group directions are inauspicious for east-group people, and the east-group directions are inauspicious for west-group people.

KUA numbers and compatibility with eight house types

KUA number	Personal Trigram	House sitting South	House sitting North	House sitting West	House sitting East	House sitting Southeast	House sitting Southwest	House sitting Northeast	House sitting Northwest
1	kan	good	best	neutral	neutral	neutral	bad	worst	bad
2	kun	worst	bad	neutral	neutral	neutral	best	good	neutral
3	chen	good	good	neutral	best	neutral	neutral	neutral	neutral
4	sun	good	good	neutral	neutral	best	worst	bad	bad
5 (men)	kun	worst	bad	neutral	neutral	neutral	best	good	neutral
5 (women)	ken	bad	bad	neutral	neutral	neutral	good	best	neutral
6	chien	bad	bad	neutral	neutral	neutral	best	good	good
7	tui	bad	bad	best	neutral	neutral	good	good	neutral
8	ken	bad	bad	neutral	neutral	neutral	good	best	neutral
9	li	best	good	neutral	neutral	neutral	bad	bad	neutral

the direct opposite of the facing direction. To determine this, take the compass direction from the front door, facing outwards. This is the *facing* direction. Then note the opposite direction. So if your house is facing east it is *sitting* west. From the sitting direction of your house and your personal KUA number you will be able to determine if the house is best, good, bad, neutral, or worst for you.

From the sitting direction of your house or apartment building, you can also draw up the Lo Shu chart of the house. This generates a set of numbers for each of the corners of the homes, which can then be used to match the annual numbers of the year. By doing this you will be able to immediately discover which corners of the home are auspicious, and which corners are dangerous in any given year. This is a simplified formula that is considered to be an excellent method for taking year-to-year readings of the home.

To use the Lo Shu chart on the following page, first determine your house sitting direction and then note its Lo Shu center number from the

second line of the chart. From this you will see at a glance which of the eight sectors of your home are afflicted by bad star numbers and which of the sectors have excellent star numbers.

Then note the years indicated in the second row. That is the year which has the same Lo Shu square as the house type indicated. In that year you will note that the sector which houses the deadly Five Yellow has become very dangerous. This is because the 5 occurs twice in the same sector in that year. In the year 2008, the Five Yellow has flown to the south which is very dangerous, since south being fire produces and strengthens the Five Yellow, an earth star. In the year 2008, however, anyone who lives in a house which has a sitting direction north, and is therefore also facing south, will have the double whammy of the Five Yellow and the Three Killings in the south. The solution is to close the door completely for that year and place loads of windchimes in the south.

For each house you can see the Three Killings and the double Five Yellow during the years indicated. But the chart also enables you to plot the luck of every house type for each of the years 2001 through to 2009. For example, in the year 2003 you can see from the chart that the Five Yellow is in the southeast, and if you live in a house that has a sitting direction of east, you will note that the illness star 2 is in the southeast. This meets the year Five Yellow and altogether makes the southeast a most dangerous sector for this house.

The year 2004 has been omitted from the chart because in that year the number in the center of the Lo shu chart is 5 and thus the deadly Five Yellow has been trapped within it. This implies that it does not have the power to bring afflictions to any of the compass sectors of that year.

You will also see that the Lo Shu center number 5 does not appear on this chart. This is because theoretically it is impossible for a house to

House types with Lo Shu numbers and annual afflictions stars

HOUSE SITTING	South	North	West	East	Southeast	Southwest	Northeast	Northwest
LO SHU center number is… also for YEAR	9 2009	1 2008	7 2002	3 2006	4 2005	2 2007	8 2001	6 2003
DANGER star 5 is in	North Five yellow	South Five yellow 3 killings	East Five yellow	West Five yellow	NW Five yellow	NE Five yellow	SW Five yellow	SE Five yellow
ILLNESS star 2 is in	West	NW	South	SE	East 3 killings	Center	NE	North
Quarrelsome star 3 is in	NE	West	North 3 killings	Center	SE	NW	South	SW
Auspicious star 8 is in	SE	East	NW	North 3 killings	South	SW	Center	West
Auspicious star 6 is in	SW	North	SE	NE	West	South	East 3 killings	Center
Auspicious star 1 is in	NW	Center	NE	East	SW	SE	West	South
Scholastic star 4 is in	South	NE	SW	NW	Center	West 3 killings	North	East
Multiplying star 9 is in	Center	SE	West	SW	North	East	NW	NE
This period lucky star 7 is in	East 3 killings	SW	Center	South	NE	North	SE	NW

have the center as its sitting direction. Given this fact, the number 5 is therefore automatically excluded.

The real value of this chart is to enable you to be forewarned of the influence of dangerous stars 5, 2, and 3, which can bring domestic havoc and misery. This illustrates one of the key principles, and the true essence of Feng Shui magic: that prevention is always better than cure.

Here we enter the realms of inner Feng Shui that tap into the connecting cord bridging earth magic with the pure essence of the mind. The mind provides invaluable help in the performance of what we term magic. Earth elements like crystals aid us in the performance of powerful magic, but it is the purification of space and mind that really leads us into uncharted territory. There are stunning bathing and meditation rituals that will take you into your deepest levels. In the process you will touch the spiritual being within you. Performing magic then becomes a part of everyday life and will not seem like magic at all – just part of the daily centering of your mind, body, and spirit with the energy patterns of the earth and sky. This kind of magic engages your mind most of all, thereby opening windows into the realms of infinity.

eight

cosmic magic of another dimension

academic success with
crystal chi

It is only with superlative grades that students qualify to study at good schools and universities and I have been asked many times whether you can arrange the Feng Shui of your children with a view to their getting better grades at school and emerging as "winners" in today's highly competitive school environments.

In this area, Feng Shui can provide some valuable help from the winds and the waters. It is possible to use straightforward earth energy to energize the northeast corners of homes and bedrooms with a view to activating wisdom luck. For adults this brings scholarly realization tinged with philosophical thought. For younger people, an energized northeast brings very good exam results.

This latter result will be more assured if you can find a crystal ball engraved with a map of the world – a crystal globe of the world so to speak. Or lapis balls, similarly engraved so they look like lapis globes. Since lapis represents the best of the earth, lapis globes are really very powerful. In fact the lapis globe can also be put into wealth vases with magnificent results. It is not necessary to buy them in very large sizes. One-inch diameter globes will do very well. Place three or four globes in the northeast to attract smooth examination luck for boys and three such globes in the northeast to benefit your daughters. If you use white crystals the same numbers also apply and again they need not be too large.

Crystal globes should not be placed on the floor but on tables in the northeast of bedrooms or the northeast of the family rooms. The added benefit of round globes is that they also signify things going smoothly with few, if any, obstacles.

You can also use an image of the double carp or *lung men* at the dragon gate. The lung men image is excellent for those about to embark on careers, perhaps those recently qualified graduates looking for jobs or training positions. This energizer works very well when used with the crystal globe of the world.

A purchased crystal should always be symbolically "cleansed" of other energies before it can tune in to the energies of your home because it will be imbued with the energy of all those who have handled the crystal before you. Simply soak it in a salt solution for 7 nights and days then clean it with a soft cloth. After this do not allow other hands to hold it. Twice a month shine a bright light into your crystal so that it is regularly activated with fresh yang energy. This will make it very powerful in attracting wisdom luck.

create magic rainbows for
happiness chi

Rainbows have many sacred meanings and connotations. Each time you see a rainbow, you should gaze at it and visualize the rainbow light entering and dissolving into your body. Create a picture in your mind of rainbow colors in a windmill formation turning in a clockwise direction on your face and your body. In your mind feel the rainbow lights activating your chakra points one at a time and then feel very relaxed. Each time you engage in the rainbow visualization you will emerge from deep meditation feeling lighter, happier, and more relaxed.

Always end your visualization with a pot of gold found at the end of the rainbow. This is such a powerful yet simple visualization, which works so fast in bringing positive results that it seems like magic.

If you find it difficult to use your mind to create rainbows in your head and body, you can hang faceted crystals near where there is bright sunshine. This

Hanging faceted crystals in your home brings in rainbows of happiness.

works really well during warm days in spring and all through summer. If you have sunny aspects in your living areas, hang faceted crystals in the windows and let the facets break the sun's light into the seven colors of the rainbow. This reflects prisms of rainbow light and brings abundant happiness chi into your home. The magic is in the effective use of sunlight chi, which is both very yang and very pure. If you succeed in introducing the sunshine into your home in this way, even killing breath is transformed into auspicious energy.

The seven colors are components of the powerful white light, and each color connects with the seven chakras of the human body, the planets of the universe, which is also regarded as heaven, and the energy spots of the earth – collectively signifying the symbolic union of heaven, earth, and humanity. There are different mantras for each of the colors and different attributes can be stimulated when we focus on each of the colors, as the house is flooded with rainbow light.

In Tibet, whenever very highly realized lamas passed away, stories would emerge about their bodies transforming into rainbow bodies – a manifestation of their holy minds attaining perfection of understanding. Or magnificent rainbows would appear in the skies that would last for several days. This was one of the signs that the highest levels of enlightenment had been attained. Indeed I have heard many stories of how when the Chinese invaded Tibet, soldiers who stormed into the meditation rooms of high lamas saw nothing but bits and pieces of hair and nails. The lamas had seemingly disappeared into thin air, having transcended this world and moved into another realm of existence. By attaining rainbow bodies they had passed on, leaving only their earthly nails and hair behind.

get rid of
negative energy
with salt and rice

Space cleansing can never be really effective without the twin mediums of salt and rice. Salt is one of the most powerful of cleansing agents while rice is a food offering to wandering earth spirits to ensure harmonious co-existence. Space clearing plays a big role in enhancing the positive in the union of positive and negative. When space is properly cleansed negative vibrations are extinguished, positive energy is enhanced, and your living space feels cleaner, brighter, and lighter. Good fortune ceases to be an illusion and becomes reality.

In Feng Shui, holding a symbolic pagoda in your left hand while sprinkling rice and salt with your right hand is believed to cause any wandering spirit with evil or bad intentions to take fright and run. The symbolic power of the pagoda is also invoked when it is incorporated into windchimes that are meant for pressing down on the bad luck of a particular corner or sector of the home.

New living space should always be cleansed, although there are several vital taboos that accompany the very

Scattering the floors of your home with rice grains and sea salt acts as a powerful cleansing ritual.

powerful rice and salt ritual. You should do this ritual only when moving into your own home, where you have a right to cleanse your space. Never attempt to use rice and salt to do space cleansing for others. You do not know the history and provenance of homes other than your own, and when you undertake the rice and salt method of cleansing for others you do not know who, in the other realms of existence, you may be disturbing or offending.

Before you begin this space-cleansing ritual, always wash your hands and face. This is useful to remember each time you undertake any spiritually-connected cleansing. It is a humble act of respect for the wandering spirits of this earth, and it ensures that you do not inadvertently offend any of them.

Walk around the external parameters of the home in a clockwise direction, throwing a mixture of raw rice grains and sea salt on the ground, at the base of the walls. Make sure you have sufficient mixture before you start. Always spend a few minutes tuning inwards and checking your motivation. Remember the purer your motivation, the more powerful you will be.

Repeat this inside the home, moving from room to room and walking in a clockwise direction around each room. Finally, at the front door, throw three handfuls from the inside outward, and then throw three handfuls from the outside into the house; don't throw too much of the mixture in each handful.

When you have finished, leave the rice and the salt on the ground until the next day before cleaning them away. Use a vacuum cleaner rather than a broom for clearing up. This is because the act of sweeping negates the good aspects of what you have done.

bathe in the magical
water of seven flowers

When you bathe in the "water of seven flowers," you become dominated by yin energy, and so set the stage for what the sages refer to as the zenith of yin. This is achieved by immersing one's entire body in water that has been activated by seven different types of auspicious flowers. This ritual bath is accompanied by a sense of increased calm and mental detachment to the surroundings.

In this wonderful bathing ritual the mind focuses on each different flower, using the petals of the flowers to frame the single, pointed thought that enables you to switch off all else. This is a powerful visualization, carried out before bathing, which allows the mind to relax, to tune into itself, and to slowly overcome all aspects of routine behavior. When you are at this stage of the process, you should cover yourself with a light robe and sit in the lotus posture, with your back straight yet calm and relaxed.

Close your eyes lightly, but do not allow yourself to doze off. The idea to is to slow down your thought processes, and let the physical body unwind and settle down. So stay tuned and focused. Never force yourself. Simply let go of unrelated thoughts and feel a sense of real and genuine freedom each time you prepare yourself for your ritualistic bath.

Flowers such as lilies, peonies, and chrysanthemums create a focus for a meditative bath ritual.

Magical bathing is one of the best ways of causing the celestial yang energy to rise forth, surrounding you with the essence of success. When activated in this way, the mind becomes your ally and Feng Shui ritual practice becomes a tool for attaining great heights of spiritual awakening.

Selecting the Flowers

Flowers for the ritual bath should be fresh, beautiful, and if possible fragrant. Jasmine and rose are intoxicating favorites, as are the lily, peony, chrysanthemum, orchid, lotus, and magnolia. In the colder months use the pink blossoms of the cherry, the peach, and the plum — which signify so many good things. Select flowers according to the seasons and where you live. There are no hard and fast rules, as long as they are freshly opened, all flowers are said to possess the yang energy required to activate the bath. You can incorporate Bach flower remedies into this bathing ritual.

Try to include in your choice of seven the colors of the five elements: white, blue or violet, red, yellow, and also deep reds to signify wood energy. This will ensure a balance of chi with no single element dominating.

The water should be made soft with bath salts, and is quite wonderful if it has been energized in sunlight for three hours. In the old days well water or natural spring water was used for ritual baths. If you can arrange for this all the better, otherwise allow tap water to stand overnight. The flowers can be put into the water whole or as petals.

Do this at least once a month, preferably followed by a spiritual purification practice. You can do any kind of practice which will make you feel cleansed and energized, but the regular calming of the mind and the cleansing of body and mind enhances your Feng Shui practices over time.

purify with incense
from high mountain herbs

You can purify a room by releasing the special essences contained within the dried leaves and twigs of high mountain herbs. When these dried mountain herbs are used as incense, fire energy releases the purity of the mountain air into your living space. When the herbs come from holy mountains the essence is far subtler, and thus operates not so much at the level of waking consciousness but affects the mind at a subliminal level.

The most famous holy mountain is probably Mount Kailash. Believed by the Hindus to be the abode of their Gods and by the Buddhists to be the pure land of their Buddha deities, Mount Kailash stands, magnificent and forbidding, on the Chinese side of the Himalayan mountains. It is said that if you can pick just a single strand of the special herbs that grow near the base of this mountain and then mix them with your pot pourri or other incense powder, it will have the power to purify a thousand lifetimes of negative karma.

The Buddhists believe that even when you reach the base of the mountain, no matter how fit you are if you do not yet have the karma to scale the heights of this holy mountain you will not be able to take even a single step forward. Yet many holy pilgrims make it to the paths of this holy mountain. Many who come by foot from Tibet make prostrations all round the mountain, as this is believed to be one of the most powerful practices for purifying eons of negative karma. For those of us who might never make it to such holy places, the next best thing is to be "bathed" in the aroma of high mountain herbs.

I have been to another holy part of the Himalayas – that of the Solu Khumbu region which is on the Nepal side of the mountain range. Here at approximately 13,000 ft (4,000 mts) above sea level there are numerous holy caves where mountain hermit lamas spent their lives mediating. Here too it is believed are hidden the precious texts buried by the highly revered Lotus Buddha, also known as Padmasambhave or Guru Rinpoche – the precious teacher.

Guru Rinpoche is credited with bringing Buddhism to Tibet, and the Tibetan holy texts speak of many scriptures hidden in this part of the Himalayas. From there comes the famous Lawado incense made from mountain herbs near the Lawado cave, home of the lawado lama who has taken rebirth in this life as Lama Zopa Rinpoche. I have the great good fortune of being a student of Lama Zopa Rinpoche and it is through knowing Rinpoche that my eyes have been opened to the wonderful purity of incense from these high mountains.

Use lawado incense, or other fragrant varieties to cleanse and purify your space.

If you can, get some of this lawado incense and burn it at least once a month to purify your space. If not, search for incense that comes from other holy mountains on other continents. The purity of the air in which they grow makes them wonderful purifying agents and burning such incense not only cleanses the space, but also creates harmony between yin and yang and amongst the different realms of consciousness.

create a "mountain of gold" mandala for the cosmos

The mountain of gold in Feng Shui has several powerful variations. The simplest version of this ritual is the creation of a symbolic mountain of gold near the main door. This is especially potent for doors that face the

You can create a symbolic golden mountain using simple rocks or small boulders painted gold. Place them outside the main door of your home.

earth or metal directions of southwest, northeast, west, and northwest. Look for some medium-sized rocks or small boulders about 6–8 in (15–20 cm) in size. Paint them a golden color and then arrange them in a mound, to symbolize a mountain, outside your entrance.

In the flying star school of Feng Shui there are several dangerous configurations of star numbers, which fly from one compass sector of the home to another, bringing intense bad luck to whichever sector they land on. The Chinese character for metal is also read as gold, hence the Feng Shui mandala practice aims at creating a golden (or metal) mountain as an antidote to the presence of severely debilitating flying stars.

The time frames of the flight of star numbers encompass all the units of time contained in Feng Shui practice. To work out where the twenty year, annual, monthly, daily, and hourly stars are at any given moment in time would be impractical, yet the bad luck caused by the coming together of bad stars all at the same time can be so severe it simply must not be ignored. I felt there had to be an easier way to deal with affliction of these troublesome stars, despite the Feng Shui having been properly put in place.

My Feng Shui colleagues and I scanned many texts on flying star Feng Shui, looking for cures and solutions, and then we discovered a very rare text on cures and remedies. The text described the golden mountain cure with great enthusiasm, and stressed that it was the most powerful cure to overcome the combinations of the deadly Five Yellow and the unlucky sickness star 2 which bring great misfortunes, loss, and illness each time they meet in any particular compass sector. The affliction is worse when the period, annual, and month stars of 5 and 2 all occur together. The discovery of the golden mountain cure was therefore a revelation, and caused great excitement.

To implement the golden mountain cure we experimented with different versions of metal mountain cures and went deep into the subject of cures for problems created by the intangible forces of time. This period of research coincided with the time I discovered the mandala offering ritual as part of my personal on-going journey into the realm of Buddhist spiritualism. I had also by then met my holy lama, who taught me the merits of making daily mandala offerings. I loved doing this practice, and found those moments when I concentrated on building my mandala very therapeutic indeed. It was only a matter of time before I realized that the mandala I held in my hand could well signify the golden mountain cure.

So I acquired additional golden mandalas filled with metal balls and semi-precious stones, and placed them in strategic corners of my home in the hope that they would overcome afflictions caused by the deadly Five Yellow and the troublesome 2 black stars. And true to expectations, troublesome work and business obstacles faded away. Commercial opportunities proceeded smoothly. Money was plentiful, despite an economic tailspin. Health improved magnificently. Persistent coughing fits and backaches were cured, and quarrels between family members petered out. These improvements to our lives made everyone at home a lot happier. You may use the living room as an area of "small place chi" and placing the mandala in corners afflicted by the Five Yellow will improve the energy enormously.

The golden mountain mandala is created by building a tiny mountain using semi-precious stones to fill special brass rings, like tiers of a cake.

In the year 2001 place the golden mountain mandala in the Southwest

In the year 2002 place it in the East

In the year 2003 place it in the Southeast

In the year 2004 place it in the Center of the house or the living room

In the year 2005 place it in the Northwest

In the year 2006 place it in the West

In the year 2007 place it in the Northeast

In the year 2008 place it in the South

The mandala offering can also be simulated by placing your hands to form elaborate hand arrangements, called hand mudras. As you visualize the golden mountain being created, place the fingers of your hands together, palms up facing you.

The mandala is created in five steps. Try it following these instructions:

1 Cross your two little fingers in front of you.

2 Place your thumbs one on top of each crossed little finger.

3 Next, invert your two second fingers to form an upright central Mount Meru.

4 Cross your two third fingers over each other.

5 Finally, place your two index fingers onto each of your two opposite third fingers.

developing concentration through
meditation

It is when the breath has become barely visible that the mind embraces it. To join the breath with the mind is the most basic, most elementary practice of meditation that will lead to a genuine emptying of the mind. When you can attain this level, you have overcome the mind's propensity to become distracted and scattered.

Meditative energy and concentrated thought is what gives power to rituals and the performance of magic. This is the eternal secret of the ancients, known to the sages and mystics of every tradition and lineage and passed orally from one generation of master practitioners to the next. Today, the process of passing on ancient secrets has changed dramatically. The written word is no longer a luxury but the widest and most easily accessible medium of instruction. Education has brought the teachings of the wise men within the reach of every person. Since perfect concentration is so vital to attaining success in the performance of Feng Shui magic, it is equally vital for practitioners to understand the essence of this practice. The better you are able to reach a point where the mind does not become distracted, the greater the success you will have in becoming a magician *par excellence.*

The key to successfully manifesting positive outcomes from all your Feng Shui rituals lies in the ability to relax, to quieten the mind, and still the passage of thoughts until you are able to imbue all your practices with precise and powerful concentration. It is then that you achieve maximum positive results.

In the early stages of your practice, keep things simple and proceed slowly with techniques that you understand and can relate to, and with benefits you can genuinely experience. Breathing meditations are ideal for calming the mind and developing the experience of insight. These are essential ingredients for successfully developing concentration.

As you start to develop your concentration, keep the sessions to no longer than ten minutes and always end your sessions while your mind and body are still fresh. Let your practice of concentration lengthen slowly. You should finish every practice session eager for more, rather than relieved it is over. Be satisfied with slow and steady progress.

Stay physically relaxed and comfortable throughout the practice sessions. Wear loose clothing, feel clean and cool, and make sure the temperature is pleasant. Later, when you have become more expert at the practice and have learnt not to be distracted by physical discomforts, you will become immune to these superficialities. But until then, incorporate anything that eases physical tensions into your practice sessions.

Remain mentally relaxed. Consciously let go of worries, problems, and the involvement of the outside world. Focus instead on the silence and quiet of your inner world. Consciously call upon memories of tranquil experiences. Recalling these occasions makes the process of attaining concentration a lot easier. Sometimes it helps if gentle music is played, as rhythmic sounds often ease the mind into a state of focused tranquility. Go with whatever works for you. When you first practice the process of relaxing your mind and body, it is easy for the mind to enter too quickly into other levels of consciousness and if you are not used to staying alert at these levels you may, at first, find that you fall asleep! But regular practice will help you stay alert.

The Meditation Sessions

To begin with, keep things simple. If you have made the decision to learn meditation in order to develop your powers of concentration it is vital to proceed at your own pace. There is no point in attempting difficult meditations before you are ready. It is also important to establish regularity of practice. You will not succeed in stilling the mind without it.

At first, practice for a few minutes increasing to perhaps 30 minutes each day, or at least several times each week. If you go for weeks without practice, you cannot expect to attain mental quieting. So, to make beneficial progress, meditate once a day at least three times a week. Discipline yourself to keep going. Once you begin to practice regularly, you will feel the benefits.

Devote a few minutes at the start of each practice session reflecting on why you are meditating. The more clearly you establish the goal of your sessions, the stronger will be your motivation, and the higher your chances of success. Make relaxation and the calming of your mind, the immediate short-term goal of your meditation. Later, as you become more adept at the practice, you can start to get more ambitious and work on developing your concentration and determination of purpose. In the beginning aim merely to subdue the mind, stilling it, gently pushing wayward thoughts out of the way.

The place where you do your practice sessions should be somewhere quiet where you will not be disturbed for the duration of your session. It is a good idea to set aside a special room that should have a comfortable temperature level.

If you find the guidelines on posture difficult or tedious, you can simply sit cross-legged and relaxed. Your mind should not be stressed by

whether you have got the posture right or wrong. Better to get it slightly wrong and be relaxed than to struggle in achieving a posture that is perfectly right but full of tension. In concentration practices, success depends very much on the ability to focus in a relaxed way.

Relaxation is the first step toward learning to meditate. Always set your intent before you begin, so you know what you want your practice to achieve.

Seven Guides to Posture in Meditation

1 **Legs:** The full lotus position with the feet placed sole upwards, on the thigh of the other leg, is recommended. This is the preferred posture of many practicing yogis or people capable of performing real magical feats that are produced by the mind's power. However, I have always meditated sitting cross-legged with both feet on the floor. Also, I find that when I place a firm cushion under the buttocks, it helps to keep my back straight, and reduces the "pins and needles" effect.

If even this posture is difficult for you, you can sit on a straight-backed chair with both feet planted firmly on the floor. You will find if you examine old pictures of the Egyptians that they are shown seated in this way. And if even this is difficult, try lying down with your back straight and your hands by your sides. This position is also acceptable. The only drawback of such a position is that you will find yourself falling asleep! When assessing posture, always be comfortable. You cannot get into a state of relaxation when your physical body is uncomfortable.

2 **Arms:** Shoulders and arms should be relaxed. This improves circulation and helps to keep you awake. As for your hands, either rest them lightly on your knees, palm downwards, or hold them loosely on your lap with the fingers aligned.

3 **Back:** The back must be straight, held relaxed but upright. It is when the back is straight that energy can easily flow through. A straight back is also conducive to longer periods of meditation. I have found that it is only when I have succeeded in staying comfortably upright that I can really feel

my mind relaxing and focusing more clearly. So make the effort to get it correct before proceeding.

4 **Eyes:** Keep you eyes lightly closed and cast downward. This enables you to shut out distractions. It is not advisable to keep your eyes too tightly closed. It is said that closing the eyes causes drowsiness but I suggest that you do whatever makes you comfortable.

For a seated meditation, sit straight-backed, with your hands on your thighs and feet flat on the floor.

5 **Mouth:** Your entire mouth and jaw should be relaxed and comfortably loose. Teeth are kept slightly apart, with lips kept lightly together.

6 **Tongue:** The tongue should be slightly touching the upper palate behind the teeth. This stops the saliva from flowing, and enables you to concentrate for longer periods.

7 **Head:** This should be naturally balanced. Do not tilt the head too far forward or backward. Hold it in such a position that your gaze can be directed naturally toward the floor in front of you. When the head position is held too high or too low, wandering thoughts can hinder concentration.

The Techniques of Meditation

There are two simple meditation techniques that I recommend for beginners who are using it to enhance their Feng Shui practice. Choose from these two methods:

- The white light meditation
- The breath consciousness method

In both methods the idea is to practice focusing the mind.

The White Light Meditation

This is a single-pointed concentration method, which achieves wonderful side benefits. To start with, white light represents the highest form of purity. It also has a wonderfully uplifting effect and makes you feel rejuvenated.

To do this, tune the mind into the presence of a brilliant white light hovering just at the edge of your consciousness. If you have difficulty picturing the white light, look directly at a bright light bulb for a few seconds before lightly closing your eyes. The image of the white light will be right before you, and you will find little difficulty then in thinking of the white light. White light meditation is something you can eventually expand into other more advanced forms of visualization.

When you first focus on the white light, you will find it relatively easy to gently disallow other thoughts from filtering through. Breathe normally. Do not hold your breath. Sit comfortably. If you like you can say gently under your breath, "I am relaxed, I am relaxed." The mind responds by obeying your thoughts. Stay focused on the white light, and gently push away any thoughts that wander into your head. Just stay relaxed and let feelings of well-being seep through.

The Breath Consciousness Meditation

This method uses conscious awareness of the breath as a way of achieving concentration and focus. It is a very popular technique taught by kung fu masters to students developing inner chi strength. Basically, the posture of meditation stays the same as the first method, but instead of focusing on white light, this technique calls for you to focus on breath awareness.

Gently breathe in and out through the nose, and follow your breath as it enters and leaves your body. Do not try to lengthen or shorten your breath at this stage. Just breathe naturally. Again when thoughts enter the mind, gently push them out while focusing on the breath.

After a while you will feel yourself beginning to melt with the relaxation that overflows into your consciousness. Watch your mind carefully. Be aware of the thoughts and feelings that enter into your consciousness. You might like to meditate on the wonder of the human breath, which is so magnificent that merely by controlling the breath, the yogi masters are able to perform feats of mental magic. The lamas of Tibet have such breathe control that they appear to be no longer breathing.

This helps to subdue the mind to an extent that inner insights start to emerge into your awareness, thereby allowing you to penetrate the inner sanctums of the mind. Later as you get better at breath consciousness, you will begin to detect the rhythm of the in breath and the out breath, which in effect allows you go deeper into your consciousness.

Over time, as you become more adept with meditation, your concentration is sure to improve and you will find that it becomes easier to focus on the key elements of Feng Shui ritualistic practice. This will enhance your incidence of success enormously.

lunar calendars

Animal	Western Calendar Dates
RAT (water)	Feb 18, 1912 – Feb 5, 1913
OX (earth)	Feb 6, 1913 – Jan 25, 1914
TIGER (wood)	Jan 26, 1914 – Feb 13 ,1915
RABBIT (wood)	Feb 14, 1915 – Feb 2, 1916
DRAGON (earth)	Feb 3, 1916 – Jan 22, 1917
SNAKE (fire)	Jan 23, 1917 – Feb 10, 1918
HORSE (fire)	Feb 11, 1918 – Jan 31, 1919
SHEEP (earth)	Feb 1, 1919 – Feb 19, 1920
MONKEY (metal)	Feb 20, 1920 – Feb 7, 1921
ROOSTER (metal)	Feb 8, 1921 – Jan 27, 1922
DOG (earth)	Jan 28, 1922 – Feb 15, 1923
BOAR (water)	Feb 16, 1923 – Feb 4, 1924

* start of 60-year Cycle

Animal	Western Calendar Dates
RAT (water)	Feb 5, 1924 – Jan 23, 1925
OX (earth)	Jan 24, 1925 – Feb 12, 1926
TIGER (wood)	Feb 13, 1926 – Feb 1, 1927
RABBIT (wood)	Feb 2, 1927 – Jan 22, 1928
DRAGON (earth)	Jan 23, 1928 – Feb 9, 1929
SNAKE (fire)	Feb 10, 1929 – Jan 29, 1930
HORSE (fire)	Jan 30, 1930 – Feb 16, 1931
SHEEP (earth)	Feb 17, 1931 – Feb 5, 1932
MONKEY (metal)	Feb 6, 1932 – Jan 25, 1933
ROOSTER (metal)	Jan 26, 1933 – Feb 13, 1934
DOG (earth)	Feb 14, 1934 – Feb 3, 1935
BOAR (water)	Feb 4, 1935 – Jan 23, 1936

Animal	Western Calendar dates
RAT (water)	Jan 24, 1936 – Feb 10, 1937
OX (earth)	Feb 11, 1937 – Jan 30, 1938
TIGER (wood)	Jan 31, 1938 – Feb 18, 1939
RABBIT (wood)	Feb 19, 1939 – Feb 7, 1940
DRAGON (earth)	Feb 8, 1940 – Jan 26, 1941
SNAKE (fire)	Jan 27, 1941 – Feb 14, 1942
HORSE (fire)	Feb 15, 1942 – Feb 4, 1943
SHEEP (earth)	Feb 5, 1943 – Jan 24, 1944
MONKEY (metal)	Jan 25, 1944 – Feb 12, 1945
ROOSTER (metal)	Feb 13, 1945 – Feb 1, 1946
DOG (earth)	Feb 2, 1946 – Jan 21, 1947
BOAR (water)	Jan 22, 1947 – Feb 9, 1948

Animal	Western Calendar dates
RAT (water)	Feb 10, 1948 – Jan 28, 1949
OX (earth)	Jan 29, 1949 – Feb 16, 1950
TIGER (wood)	Feb 17, 1950 – Feb 5, 1951
RABBIT (wood)	Feb 6, 1951 – Jan 26, 1952
DRAGON (earth)	Jan 27, 1952 – Feb 13, 1953
SNAKE (fire)	Feb 14, 1953 – Feb 2, 1954
HORSE (fire)	Feb 3, 1954 – Jan 23, 1955
SHEEP (earth)	Jan 24, 1955 – Feb 11, 1956
MONKEY (metal)	Feb 12 ,1956 – Jan 30, 1957
ROOSTER (metal)	Jan 31, 1957 – Feb 17, 1958
DOG (earth)	Feb 18, 1958 – Feb 7, 1959
BOAR (water)	Feb 8, 1959 – Jan 27, 1960

Animal	Western Calendar dates
RAT (water)	Jan 28, 1960 – Feb 14, 1961
OX (earth)	Feb 15, 1961 – Feb 4, 1962
TIGER (wood)	Feb 5, 1962 – Jan 24, 1963
RABBIT (wood)	Jan 25, 1963 – Feb 12, 1964
DRAGON (earth)	Feb 13, 1964 – Feb 1, 1965
SNAKE (fire)	Feb 2, 1965 – Jan 20, 1966
HORSE (fire)	Jan 21, 1966 – Feb 8, 1967
SHEEP (earth)	Feb 9, 1967 – Jan 29, 1968
MONKEY (metal)	Jan 30, 1968 – Feb 16, 1969
ROOSTER (metal)	Feb 17, 1969 – Feb 5, 1970
DOG (earth)	Feb 6, 1970 – Jan 26, 1971
BOAR (water)	Jan 27, 1971 – Feb 14, 1972
RAT (water)	Feb 15, 1972 – Feb 2, 1973
OX (earth)	Feb 3, 1973 – Jan 22, 1974
TIGER (wood)	Jan 23, 1974 – Feb 10, 1975
RABBIT (wood)	Feb 11, 1975 – Jan 30, 1976
DRAGON (earth)	Jan 31, 1976 – Feb 17, 1977
SNAKE (fire)	Feb 18, 1977 – Feb 6, 1978
HORSE (fire)	Feb 7, 1978 – Jan 27, 1979
SHEEP (earth)	Jan 28, 1979 – Feb 15, 1980
MONKEY (metal)	Feb 16, 1980 – Feb 4, 1981
ROOSTER (metal)	Feb 5, 1981 – Jan 24, 1982
DOG (earth)	Jan 25, 1982 – Feb 12, 1983
BOAR (water)	Feb 13, 1983 – Feb 1, 1984

Animal	Western Calendar dates
* start of 60-year Cycle	
RAT (water)	Feb 2, 1984 – Feb 19, 1985
OX (earth)	Feb 20, 1985 – Feb 8, 1986
TIGER (wood)	Feb 9, 1986 – Jan 28, 1987
RABBIT (wood)	Jan 29, 1987 – Feb 16, 1988
DRAGON (earth)	Feb 17, 1988 – Feb 5, 1989
SNAKE (fire)	Feb 6, 1989 – Jan 26, 1990
HORSE (fire)	Jan 27, 1990 – Feb 14, 1991
SHEEP (earth)	Feb 15, 1991 – Feb 3, 1992
MONKEY (metal)	Feb 4, 1992 – Jan 22, 1993
ROOSTER (metal)	Jan 23, 1993 – Feb 9, 1994
DOG (earth)	Feb 10, 1994 – Jan 30, 1995
BOAR (water)	Jan 31, 1995 – Feb 18, 1996
RAT (water)	Feb 19, 1996 – Feb 6, 1997
OX (earth)	Feb 7, 1997 – Jan 27, 1998
TIGER (wood)	Jan 28, 1998 – Feb 15, 1999
RABBIT (wood)	Feb 16, 1999 – Feb 4, 2000
DRAGON (earth)	Feb 5, 2000 – Jan 23, 2001
SNAKE (fire)	Jan 24, 2001 – Feb 11, 2002
HORSE (fire)	Feb 12, 2002 – Jan 31, 2003
SHEEP (earth)	Feb 1, 2003 – Jan 21, 2004
MONKEY (metal)	Jan 22, 2004 – Feb 8, 2005
ROOSTER (metal)	Feb 9, 2005 – Jan 28, 2006
DOG (earth)	Jan 29, 2006 – Feb 17, 2007
BOAR (water)	Feb 18, 2007 – Feb 6, 2008

index